Light & Dark

Selected Columns
1987-1997
by
Eric Rush

From the
Peninsula Daily News
Port Angeles, Washington

Price: $10

Light & Dark

Published February 1999

Western Gull Publishing
Book Division of the *Peninsula Daily News*
P.O. Box 1330
Port Angeles WA 98362

ISBN 0-9610910-5-3

Printed by Olympic Printers—Port Angeles, Washington

For my mother who died too soon

And for my father

Introduction

Early in 1987. Anton Wishik, then managing editor of the *Peninsula Daily News*, asked if I'd like to write a weekly column. He knew me only from a couple of published letters and a story in Peninsula College's literary magazine, *Tidepools.* I thought it over for maybe half a second.

What should I write about? Whatever I wanted, but don't pontificate on national and international affairs. The newspaper gets George Will and Ellen Goodman for the same price they get me.

How do I decide what to write about? Whatever injustice or outrage is making me mad as deadline approaches, whatever provoked my brain or touched my heart in preceding days, whatever misadventure might be worth your while to spend a few minutes reading about. Some weeks I can't think of anything until I sit down and start writing, and some weeks, not even then. At times when I feel completely burned out and consider quitting, someone will pay me the highest of compliments: I like reading your column, even when I don't agree with you.

I've resisted the urge to rewrite some of these, but I've made a few changes in wording to improve clarity and to correct minor errors. Any errors that remain are mine alone.

I disagree with some established rules of capitalization and punctuation, and I've indulged myself in this book.

In spite of a familial and educational background in English, I have never been able to sense when to use 'who' and when to use 'whom'. I can't find any good reason for preserving both forms. I don't use 'whom' unless my ear won't let me do otherwise. I urge you to do the same.

The columns in this collection are not in strict chronological order and are not grouped by theme or subject. I've tried in my column to balance from week to week the serious with the frivolous, the light with the dark. This book should reflect that.

There is one thread that runs throughout. This book begins and ends with my dog. Readers of the *Peninsula Daily News* knew Buddy from his beginning to his end, and his epitaph touched more hearts than I'd have thought possible.

Eric Rush
Sequim, Washington

Light & Dark

Buddy: the beginning

If an astrologer had told me a few years ago that I would get a dog in 1988, I'd have laughed.   If the stargazer had said I'd buy one, with real money, I'd have laughed even harder and given him Nancy Reagan's phone number.

I've always had a cat or two. They're relatively quiet and they don't pester you for attention the way dogs do. Most dogs are like most other people's kids: No manners.

When Katrina decided she wanted a dog, I resisted, but eventually she wore ol' Dad down.   Even I could see it wasn't fair to expect other members of the family to embrace my prejudices, so we got her a puppy named Stephanie from an acquaintance who was moving out of town.

It wasn't long before I found out why most dogs don't have good manners. It's the same reason other people's kids don't: Nobody teaches them.

We taught Stephanie the usual sit-stay-come routine. We also tried to teach her not to jump on people, but she's smart enough to figure out who she can get away with jumping on and who she can't. She never jumps on me, though. Very smart dog.

She has a pillow in a corner of the living room. If she gets in the way, we send her to her pillow. It works fine.

The steps to our back door are narrow and steep. To have a dog come charging between or past our legs while we're struggling up the steps with groceries could be disastrous, so we taught the dog never to go through the door without being invited.

Stephanie took that a step further than we'd intended. She recognized a wooden gate in a barbed-wire fence as a door. She'll run under the wire beside the open gate without hesitation, but she won't walk through the gate uninvited.

So I was wrong. Having a dog in the family isn't bad at all. Even the cats don't mind. But I didn't want one of my own.

I changed my mind. Birds changed my mind. Grouse and pheasant and quail changed my mind.

I've come late to the sport of hunting upland birds, but I've come quickly to the realization that hunting birds without a dog is like going on a picnic alone. Both are far more enjoyable with company.

I've been telling myself for a couple of seasons that I should get a bird dog. In addition to the pleasure of watching the dog work, there is the satisfaction of knowing that the dog will find crippled birds that I might not.

So I did what I always do when I embark on something new. went to the library and started reading books on dogs. I talked to friends who hunt with dogs, and I hunted with them and their dogs.

I've liked the looks of English Setters for as long as I can remember. A man I know owns an exceptionally beautiful one bred of good hunting stock. He told me who he bought it from and I gave the breeder a call. He said a litter was on the way.

Last week, I saw the pups. Eight of them. Five weeks old.

I have no idea what the chemistry is that causes a person to pick a specific pup from a litter. Although I watched them all run and play and nurse and sleep, my eye kept returning to one.

At five weeks, the puppies don't seem to grasp the concept of edges. They run off the edge of the patio and fall on their faces in the grass a foot or so below. Put them back on the patio, and soon they fall off again.

But not all of them. The one I liked best fell off once. I picked him up and set him back from the edge. He ran toward the same place where he'd gone over and I got ready to stop him, but he slowed, waked to the edge, and carefully looked down as if trying to figure out what had happened. That was good enough for me.

My dog comes home in two weeks. I hope my cat understands.

never know what to do . . .

I never know what to do about the beggars.

Unless we spend time on the sidewalks of large cities, we have the luxury of deciding how we should respond to panhandlers based on theoretical ethics and the moralities instilled in our upbringing. It's not so easy when you look into the eyes behind the outstretched palms.

Christian morality says, if I have two coats and meet someone with none, I should give him one of mine. But what if I have two coats and meet a hundred people with none?

Those whose thinking is unswayed by feeling say we should not give to beggars, that it only encourages them. They liken giving handouts to people to feeding wild animals begging beside the road and argue that, in the long run, doing so does more harm than good.

It's tempting to compare person-to-person handouts to government welfare programs, handouts on a national scale. But making such comparisons sometimes yields surprises. What are we to make of a person who opposes welfare but is the first to offer his hand to a neighbor in need? What of a professed humanitarian who favors government welfare programs but does not see the needy in his own back yard?

We can theorize all we want, but theories not tempered by reality aren't worth much. Large-scale welfare programs are not the same as dealing with individual beggars in person.

If I were to encounter a panhandler on the streets of Sequim, it would be so unusual that I'd want to talk to him, find out who he is, where he's from, and what circumstances require him to beg. But not in New York.

Some big-city beggars panhandle because they make good livings at it. They set their own hours, answer to no boss, and pay no income taxes. Some smile and speak politely and take rejection without bitterness. Others are sullen and too drunk or stoned to work, even if they were otherwise qualified. Perhaps they get enough to live on without going to the trouble of engaging in any way with those who might toss a quarter into their grubby cups. Some grin above signs saying they want money for beer. But others need a few bucks just to eat each day, and there is no easy way to tell the difference between them. Each one successfully ignored makes it a little easier to ignore them all.

Street musicians are, to my mind, a better class of beggar. They perhaps retain some pride and preserve it by exchanging music for money. Perhaps they pretend that they are not begging, and perhaps they are not. I don't even try to ignore them. A dollar or two in the hat at the violinist's feet is not a large price to pay to help preserve someone's dignity.

Beggars in poor countries are another matter. Small Mexican children trying to sell useless handmade trinkets on the sidewalk break my heart, but to give one of them a few pesos in sight of others brings an overwhelming horde in seconds. They know all Anglos are rich, and they try very hard to separate us from just a little of our wealth.

Older children move through the marketplace from foreigner to foreigner, ignoring their own who also ignore them. They launch into spiels in fragmented English, tales of woe and need.

Sharing wealth is a fine, noble idea, but Communism demonstrated that forcing the rich to share wealth equally instead spreads poverty equally. There are already far too many people on earth to share its limited and diminishing wealth. An equal division would reduce the few nations that are rich to poverty and would not raise the many that are poor enough to make any difference.

But knowing this in my brain does not help the ache in my heart when I, with a good meal in my belly and a good shirt on my back, see a very young woman sitting on a narrow sidewalk with a small child at her feet and an infant at her breast, a hand held out to all who pass and a silent plea in her eyes. It does not help when I walk past little children whose eyes are almost as empty as their stomachs and hands, and I wonder how there can be any hope for them and for their children to come.

Reasonable doubt

The trial didn't make the front page. It was the kind of routine traffic case that usually is settled with a ticket and a fine, not by a jury's verdict. But it was an important trial. It was important to the defendant because to be found guilty of a felony hit and run would mark her forever. It was important to me because I was serving on a jury for the first time.

There were six of us, four men and two women.

It seemed simple enough on the face of it. The defendant was backing her small car out of a parking space and allegedly ran her front bumper into the side of a car next to hers. Witnesses parked next to the struck car on the other side saw it move. They saw the defendant pull forward into the parking space again, and then back out. The defendant noticed the witnesses watching her, shrugged, and drove away.

The defendant's contention was that she was not aware she'd hit the other car. The law says, if she didn't know she hit it, she was not guilty of hit and run.

She said she was looking over her shoulder as she started backing out, then looked forward and saw she was too close to the other car, pulled forward to try again, and backed out. When she saw several people watching her inept job of unparking, she shrugged in embarrassment and drove away.

I was surprised that our first ballot wasn't unanimous. Four of us voted to acquit.

After some discussion of the testimony and of what constitutes reasonable doubt, the vote was still four to two, but now favoring conviction. How could anyone hit a parked car and not know it?

The two holding out for acquittal were a man in his sixties and me. We argued for hours. The vote did not change. We asked for specific information on reasonable doubt. The judge wouldn't help us. I called home and told Barb I'd be late for my birthday dinner.

I argued that we did not have enough information to know beyond a reasonable doubt that the defendant knew she hit the car. We did not know how much the struck car moved or in what manner it moved. Was it a sharp lurch or a gentle motion? Was the damage a shallow crease or a deep gouge? Would the plastic bumper make noise against the side of the car? We did not know.

The defendant's explanation was not unreasonable. It was not inconsistent with the sparse facts we, the jury, were privy to. Since the prosecution had not presented evidence that its version of events was the only reasonable version, it was obvious to me that the case had not been proved beyond a reasonable doubt. The defendant might be guilty, but she might be innocent. Ties go to the runner. Draws go to the champion. Innocent until proven guilty.

Two of us insisted that we could not assume that the damage was so great or the motion so abrupt that the defendant had to have known she hit the car. If that were the case, the prosecutor should have made us aware of them.

We were deadlocked. It was a tired and hungry jury that was released long after sundown. The case was not retried.

I talked with the man who had held out with me and we discovered we had something in common. We had both been involved in false accusations when we were children. In both situations, all the "facts" pointed toward guilt.

He had been accused of stealing a neighbor's purse. I had accused a playmate of stealing my wallet during a scuffle over who was going to pay for a window broken in a snowball fight.

I *knew* my friend was guilty. He had his hand in my back pocket while we fought, the argument was over money, and my wallet turned up missing soon after. I had more evidence against him than the prosecution had on the defendant in that trial.

The other man's neighbor found her purse where she'd misplaced it. I found my wallet on the table beside my bed where I'd put it the night before.

Urban beachcombing

You don't need to live anywhere near water to enjoy beach-combing. You can enjoy the same leisurely walking with eyes cast down and darting from object to object in hopes of finding something valuable on the "beach" of sand and gravel between the pavement and the ditch along roads and highways everywhere.

I started urban beachcombing early. As a six-year-old, I cruised residential alleys with friends and found all manner of broken toys and small appliances waiting for the trash hauler.

When I was twelve, the favored find along roads was smokable cigaret butts. Pickings were always slim for several days after a rain, but during a long dry spell, we could afford to be picky about brands.

You won't find glass fishnet floats from Japan along the road. What you'll find more than anything else is nails. Ordinary everyday nails. I don't know where they come from, but there they are, all sizes and types, new and old, along streets and highways.

When you begin roadway beachcombing, you might have the impulse to pick up the nails to keep them out of someone's tires, but unless you want the nails, don't bother. There are so many of them that trying to pick them all up is drudgery, not fun.

Second most common are steel washers. Most of them probably fall off cars and trucks, but they are far more common than nuts and bolts. Since the nuts or bolt or both have to fall off before the washers can, why are there so few?

Light & Dark

I pick up washers. I also pick up nuts and bolts. It's not as practical picking up nuts and bolts as it is washers because you end up with dozens of nuts and dozens of bolts and few of them go together.

Along with the washers and nuts and bolts, you sometimes find the parts they used to hold onto the cars and trucks. Usually it's some unidentifiable clamp or bracket than can fall off without alerting the driver to its absence. And, although wheel bolts are nearly as common as bottle caps, I've never found a wheel.

I have a friend who melts down lead and casts bullets. One prime source of lead is wheel counterweights, those curved pieces of lead that mechanics hammer onto rims when they balance wheels. So I've started picking up wheel weights.

The first thing you'll notice if you pick up weights is, there are almost none along low-speed roads. If one is going to come off it's most likely to come off at high speed. The second thing you'll notice is, the weight of lead adds up fast.

The best thing to find is money. Every now and then somewhere in the country, the door of an armored car flies open and a bag of money falls out and scatters. Cars screech to a halt and people leap out to grab as much cash as the can, and who knows how much they miss? I keep my eyes peeled for rolls of quarters and bundles of twenties, but what I find is pennies.

The reason it's pennies is that most people won't go to the trouble of picking them up. My philosophy on pennies is derived from Ben Franklin's: Finding one is more fun than earning one.

I had a day to kill in San Francisco, so I went for a walk. I left the airport before breakfast and got back at dusk. I had no map and no clear idea of where I was after the first ten miles or so, but it didn't matter. I followed streets and highways and trails and I passed up more than I picked up. It was like eating M&Ms; a few are a treat, but too many is too much.

Even so, it was a good day. I ended up with a couple of pounds of lead weights, three dozen washers, several nuts and bolts (including a matched pair), a small spring, a marble-sized ball bearing, two packs of matches, a Wilson #1 tennis ball, a Ticonderoga #2 pencil, and six cents cash. I also had sore feet and a sunburn, but I felt better than I would have had I sat around the hotel and watched TV. I also have a sackful of valuable loot.

10

Iearts of hunters, big and small

Even though recent days have been Summer hot, something in the air feels like Autumn. Animals sense it and begin to do e things they do to get ready for Winter. Dark green leaves ;hten and begin to yellow. Late garden produce begins to ripen, id I respond to an unconscious urge to cut firewood, even ough I have more than enough on hand for two Winters.

t's almost time to put trout tackle away, but I'll wait awhile; the ools of river water when the level is low, reflecting golden light at filters through yellowing leaves, are difficult to resist.

Hunting seasons begin to open this month, and I find myself, ice again, wishing I'd been more diligent through the year in acticing with shotgun and bow, that I'd—

"Wait a minute! You mean you're one of those brutes who goes it with guns and murders defenseless animals? I thought you re a liberal!"

(Here we go again.)

Slow down a minute. If you want to argue, make up your mind iat you want to argue about—guns, hunting, or political ilosophy.

"Guns, hunting, what's the difference? You go out and murder iimals with guns. That's hunting."

'our misplaced passion betrays your ignorance. Murder is traspecific. People can murder only other people.

"Yeah, sure. You'd rather call it 'harvesting' or something ually innocuous."

11

Wrong again. I know most people shy away from the word and the idea of killing, but, ultimately, the object of hunting is killing and there's nothing wrong with saying so.

"But why do you hunters do it? Why do you go out with gun and kill things?"

There's more to hunting than killing. If killing were the only thing, we'd keep wild animals in pens and simply kill them as we do cattle in a slaughterhouse.

You keep mentioning hunting and guns together, but that limits your perception of hunting. I hunt birds with a shotgun, deer and elk with bow and arrow, trout with a fly rod, and all of them with a camera. I spend lots of quiet hours in the woods before hunting season, looking for animal sign and trying to learn their routines.

"So you can kill 'em later."

Yes, maybe. If I'm skillful and lucky. But, for most hunters especially older ones, the kill isn't the most important thing.

All that time in the woods is time I'm not sitting in a chair or car seat. It's time to let my mind rest from everyday matters, to let it ramble where it will and think what it wants to think.

If killing animals were the important thing, why would we make hunting so difficult? The easy and efficient ways to kill game animals are illegal. The best time to hunt deer is at night with spotlight, but that's illegal and generally considered unsporting. Bird hunters have limits on shotgun size and ammunition capacity. It's easier to catch trout with bait than with lures, so some waters are reserved for flies and spinners.

"Fishing's different."

Is it? Sport fishing involves the same elements as hunting. Fishermen need to know the habits of their prey as much as hunters do. Fishermen stalk animals in their habitat with the object of killing them. The main difference is, fish don't have soft fur and warm brown eyes. Bambi wasn't a trout.

"Yeah, but a lot of fishermen don't kill what the catch. They let 'em go."

That's my point. The hunt is more important than the kill.

"If that's all there is to it, why not just go off in the woods and watch animals? Why bother hunting at all?"

Why indeed?

And why do kittens chase butterflies?

ccentric, or just plain wrong?

When someone asked me why I write dates in day/month/year order instead of the conventional, to nericans, month/ day/year, I explained that most of the world es it that way. It's more logical to work in one direction, from nall to large units of time, than to start in the middle with the onth. And writing today's date 9 October 1992 eliminates the uttering comma.

've adopted several unusual conventions over the years. I can t away with calling them conventions because my hair is aying. If I were half my age, they would be errors.

Confusion arises between Europeans and us when we use imbers to designate months and the day is numbered 12 or wer. 10/9/92 is October 9 in this country and 10 September sewhere. Halloween's date of 31/10/92 is obviously in day/onth/year order.

n my journals, I use 24-hour time. Flight logs are kept in iilitary" time, too. It eliminates the colon and the a.m. or p.m. st of all, it eliminates 12:00a.m. and 12:00p.m., both of which use confusion and argument. With a 24-hour clock, the only ing left to argue about is whether the minute after 2359 is 2400 0000.

ome airline schedules solve the twelve o'clock problem by rrectly indicating Noon or Midnight for flights departing at ose times. Others show departures at 11:59 or 12:01.

Newspapers and magazines use stylebooks to create conformity the mechanics of writing. I noticed some time ago that my yle has changed in writing this column to avoid conflict with nvention.

Light & Dark

I capitalize the names of the seasons. Summer and Winter present no problem uncapitalized, but Spring and Fall mean to many other things. Does the phrase "After the fall" refer to a time of year or a time after an accident?

We don't capitalize "month", but we do the names of the months. I like to treat seasons the same way, but stylebooks won't let me. So in my column, I refer to the season after Summer as autumn and try to avoid reference to the one that comes after Winter.

Why "till" became the accepted and even preferred contraction for 'until' is beyond my comprehension. I prefer "'til", but I use the whole word to avoid having it changed. The sentence, "We can't till the till till there's something in the till," makes perfect sense, but not 'til you figure out which till is which.

Items in a written series are set off by commas, but intellectual battles rage over the use of the comma before the conjunction. Modern convention discards it. I like it for the rhythm it imparts. To my ear, our flag is red, white, and blue. It is not red, whiteandblue.

Writing authority Jan Venolia advocates using the serial comma to avoid ambiguity. Consider what the absence of that final comma does in Venolia's illustration: "Clean sheets, the smell of freshly baked bread and my kid sister all remind me of home."

Most modern publications dispense with the final comma. I get around that by avoiding the series: Our flag is red and white. It is also blue.

If the title enclosed in quotation marks appears at the end of the sentence, I want the period outside the quotation mark because the period is not part of the title. Convention places the period within the quotation, although any other sentence-ending punctuation would fall outside it: I liked "War and Peace." Did you read "War and Peace"?

I think the period was moved inside the quotation by early printers to keep the isolated dot from breaking off the bar of type metal. With that kind of printing obsolete, maybe it's time to move it back outside.

As I write this, it's 1100 on 6 October. My flight leaves at 1950 from Seattle and I need to be at the airplane by 1830, so I'd better pack my bag comma take this column to the *Daily News* comma and head for Seattle.

14

Deprived...of television?

A friend told me the other day that, now that his two children are of school age, he and his wife are starting to get pressure from other parents, well-meaning people in their church and neighborhood who think their two children are deprived.

Both kids are bright and healthy. The first-grader reads several years above her age level. The kindergartner also reads. When they aren't reading or playing with other kids, they have plenty of things to do at home. The whole family plays board games together, and the kids have their own interests—drawing and painting, make-believe games with dolls and toys, and construction project with blocks and Tinkertoys and Legos.

Yep, those kids are deprived, all right. They don't have television. Never have had one. They don't get to sit with glazed eyes and blank expressions while the box pours murder, mayhem, cheap sex, and laugh tracks into their young minds.

Oh, but what about the good programs?

Good programs for six-year-olds? Like what—cartoons?

Oh, *Sesame Street*. Programs like that probably do some kids some good, kids who have spent so much time watching TV that they need some form of Head Start program to try to catch up to where they would be if they hadn't had TV in the first place.

And, even though there are some worthwhile TV shows, programs with greater value than passive "entertainment," there are so few that having a television set in the house to watch them

15

is like keeping a can of garbage in the living room because it might contain a few edible turnips.

Steve Allen, of all people, said in a 1983 newspaper interview that Americans had grown dumber in the preceding twenty-five years. "College entrance scores make it very clear," he said. And he blamed it on TV—"junk food for the mind."

Watching television wastes time that could be spent reading. People who watch TV and don't learn to read learn far less than people who read and don't watch TV. It's not just a matter of content, either. The act of reading exercises the mind and imagination; television numbs them.

That it prevents children from learning how to learn is reason enough to keep TV out of the house, but it does worse than that.

Herbert London, in a commentary in the *New York Times*, described how young people absorb the moral values of the characters they watch on TV. They think that the way the characters on *Dynasty* or *Dallas* view the world and act within it is normal behavior. They don't see anything wrong with lying and cheating to get what they want because it works on TV.

London quoted from Bruno Bettelheim's opinions of television: "...it deals in stereotypes, and that is devastating to the intelligent development of young people. Television characters go through life unchanged by their experiences. [Children] lose the ability to learn from reality because life experiences are more complicated than the ones they see on screen and there is no one who comes in at the end to explain it all."

So whose kids are deprived?

Now that Christmas is near, my friends have noticed a difference between their two children and their classmates. The other kids have long wish lists. They want every expensive batteries-not-included toy that TV commercials have to offer. Many of those things are like television itself: You don't do anything *with* them; you turn them on and *watch* them.

My friends' little boy wants more Legos. That's all. He wants Legos because he likes to build things, to create things with them.

The little girl? She wants two things. She wants a long white dress and a telescope.

Yep, those kids are deprived, all right. Not only are they being denied the opportunity to deaden their minds and twist their moral outlooks, they've been denied the joys of greed.

The nature of friendship

Funny how a friendship can grow, even though there seems to be little for it to grow on.

I met Jeff in Colorado in sixth grade. He was a new kind in school, fresh from California. He was clean cut and he went to Sunday school every week. He and I used to sneak off the school grounds during recess to smoke cigarets and Red Dot cigars.

He talked me into going to Sunday school with him. If I'd go to his once, he'd go to mine.

His church was more formal than the Unitarian style of worship I was accustomed to. His teacher put me on the spot by asking me to recite the books of the New Testament. I didn't know where to begin. I explained that at my church we were studying Buddhism that month, so I wasn't too sharp on the New Testament.

The next week, Jeff wouldn't come to Sunday school with me. He didn't want to miss out on Mark or Luke or whoever was up that week. I felt I'd been snookered, but Jeff and I stayed friends throughout the year. Then his family moved back to California and I didn't see him again until he returned to Colorado in our junior year of high school.

I noticed him, but I didn't recognize him. Everybody noticed him. He was pure California hotrod cool. He had the longest, greasiest DA haircut in the school with a full-curl waterfall in front. His Levis were so low on his hips that his billfold banged the back of his knee when he walked. The steel horseshoe taps on his heels clanked in the halls like a blacksmith's hammer. I wasn't sure it was Jeff until the teacher called the roll.

Jeff wasn't sure he recognized me, either. That was the year went without a haircut for six months on a fifty-cent bet.

We were glad to see each other, but we weren't exactly th buddies we'd been in grade school. Jeff ran with the hotro crowd and I barely knew a camshaft from a four-eleven rear end He moved back to California for his last year of high school and didn't hear from him again for ten years.

And again I didn't recognize him immediately. His appearanc was more like it was in sixth grade and he wore glasses. For tha matter, so did I. We were both back in Colorado, working in grocery store, after ten years of marriages, divorces, and othe adventures and misadventures.

He'd married right out of high school, had children an divorced, married and divorced again. I was married for th second time. Neither of us had spent much time in college and at an age when most men are well established in careers, both c us were still drifting from one kind of job to another, quick t learn new jobs and easily bored by them.

Fifteen years ago, I moved to Port Angeles and all but lost trac of Jeff again. I'd write once a year or so, and he'd call about a often, sometimes from California, sometimes from Colorad Once he drifted out this way and stopped to visit. Once I saw hir in Santa Rosa.

Funny thing happened to Jeff a few years ago. He got marrie again. To his original wife. To the grandmother of his grand children. I met Beth last year when the three of us met in Sa Francisco for dinner. They don't look like grandparents. They'r too young. They're *my* age.

We met again a couple of weeks ago, in Colorado this time. Jef is starting a career in aviation at the age of forty-six. Aviatio doesn't bore him. It doesn't bore me either.

We had dinner with my parents. Dad told some of his treasur of stories about his childhood on a farm in Texas. Jeff and I tol stories about our childhoods that parents should never hear unt their children are grown.

During a lull in laughter, Beth said, "Now I see why these guy have been friends for so long. Their brains work the same way."

Maybe that's it. Maybe the core of friendship is a recognition deep in our minds, of similarity. Maybe what we see and love ir our friends is ourselves.

Small-town boy in the big city

When the woman offered me a cut-rate to a Broadway musical, I politely declined. I might be from the hick side of the Hudson, but I ain't that stupid. I've heard of the old fake-ticket scam, you see.

I was on weekend layover in New York City for the first time in several months. After spending Saturday walking around and seeing the sights, I was sitting at the counter in a café on Broadway, a few blocks north of the theater district. I was reading a book as I ate and didn't notice the man and woman at a table nearby. But they noticed me.

They were right behind me when I paid my bill. I don't know how they knew I was from out of town. Maybe they saw the street map sticking out of my pocket.

"Excuse me," she said.

I turned around.

"We noticed you were alone. We have one extra ticket to a play tonight. A musical. Would you like to go?"

They didn't look like crooks. They looked like grandparents. But swindlers never look like swindlers.

"No thank you," I said. "I'm not dressed for something like that." I was wearing faded jeans and running shoes.

The woman kept taking while I put on my hat and jacket and the man with her paid their bill.

"Don't worry about it," she said. "Lots of people go casual. They won't turn you away."

"Well," I said and looked at my watch, "What time does it start? Where is it? What's the name of it?" As we talked, we moved out into the sidewalk.

"It's called *Mail*. It starts at eight at the Music Box Theater on Forty-fifth."

The theater was a block from my hotel. I'd have time to walk to the hotel, change clothes, and make it to the theater in time. If the ticket was good and if I wanted to pay half or of the regular forty- or fifty-dollar price. Which I didn't.

"Thank you for asking me, but I'd probably better skip it and get some sleep." I explained that I was airline crew on layover. I didn't mention I wasn't leaving for two days.

"That's too bad," the man said. "We saw it last week and everybody loved it. Except the critics, of course."

"That's right," the woman said. "Our senior citizen center gets tickets free. Sometimes we have extras that we sell to friends for the three-dollar service charge we have to pay. But it's so difficult to give away just one ticket. That's why, when we saw you by yourself, we thought maybe you'd like to go."

Three bucks? Only *three bucks*? I could afford to get stung for three bucks.

"Only three bucks?" I asked. We were standing on a corner waiting for the light.

"Yes, that's all." She pulled a ticket from her purse. "Are you sure you can't go?"

"Maybe I should," I said. "I've never been to a Broadway show."

I'd probably be in the back row of the balcony behind a post, but what do you want for three bucks?

I gave her the money and she gave me the ticket. They turned at the next corner and I thanked them. They said I was welcome and they hoped I'd enjoy it and, by the way, don't mention to the theater people how I got the ticket. They weren't really supposed to give the extras away.

When I got to my hotel room, I examined the ticket. It looked okay to me, but how was I to know? Instead of listing a price, it said "Complimentary."

I changed clothes and got to the theater a couple of minutes before curtain time. I was nervous when I handed the man my ticket. I half expected him to recognize it as a senior citizen ticket and challenge me, but of course he didn't.

I had a good seat on an aisle and thoroughly enjoyed myself. I'd like to write to the couple who talked me into going to tell them how much I enjoyed it, but I didn't think to ask their names.

Buddy: raising pups and kids

The biggest difference between bringing home a new baby and bringing home a new puppy is in who gets stuck with the work.

A puppy doesn't have to be a lot of work. I could get this column written faster if I didn't have to stop every minute or so to take a dictionary out of the pup's mouth and replace it with his shoe. I could put him out in his kennel and let him howl until he's exhausted. What the heck, a lot of people raise children pretty much that way.

But that's not the way I was raised, not the way my daughter was raised, and not the way my pup will be raised, either.

The first night might have gone easier if we'd gotten him home before ten o'clock at night. Maybe he'd have had time to get used to his new home and had time to adjust to not having seven other pups to sleep with. We might have had time to learn the subtle signals that forecast wetness with accuracy the weather service might envy.

One of us had final exams the next day, one had to get up and go to work and that left me to take care of the pup so the rest of the family could sleep. That was only fair. It's my dog.

As my parents' generation turned to Benjamin Spock to learn how to cope with human babies, I turned to Richard Wolters: "Whoever takes the place of the mother will be very important to the dog." I guess that's me.

So I got an old shirt out of the dirty clothes, one full of sweat and smell, settled the pup on it in front of the wood stove, lay down on the carpet beside him, and we went to sleep.

21

Light & Dark

Like a mother with a new baby, the slightest whine or whimper brought me fully awake. Often. And like a new mother, I didn't get much sleep. The rest of the family did, though, and so did the pup. I had to get up only four times to take him outside. I should have gotten up five times, but it didn't take long to learn which whimpers mean, "Feed me," "Pet me," or "Where are my brothers and sisters?" and the important one that means, "You've got ten seconds to get me outside, Boss."

The second night was easier. I got to sleep in bed.

Pup and I had gone to the pet store and got him one of those plastic airline pet carriers. Now he has only one sleeping place to get used to, one place all his own.

He didn't like it at first, but if I waited until he was sleepy enough to fall over, I could put him in it on my old shirt with his rawhide chew and an old tennis shoe, pet him for a few seconds and he'd fall asleep. After a couple of days, he started going in there for naps on his own.

One advantage of a small kennel or cage is that the dog will try hard to keep it dry. He doesn't much care about the living room carpet; he can soak half of it down and still have room to play and sleep. Besides, the carpet isn't his.

The second night pup was home, he slept in his kennel beside the bed. I dangled an arm over the side and stuck my fingers through the grill and slept that way. When he woke up lonesome he'd lick my fingers and go back to sleep. If he needed to go out he'd stay dry and whimper until I got up and carried his kennel outside and let him out. I got more sleep that night. On the third night, I didn't even have to leave my fingers in the cage.

Life with pup is going well. There's extra work to do, same as with a baby. And somebody has to pay him lots of attention. Speaking of which, this little critter that I cleverly tired out by letting him sit on my lap and gnaw my wrists while I tried to type is awakening from his nap at my feet. I'll take him for a walk in the wide, wide world, and then he'll sleep for a couple of hours. Maybe three, if I'm lucky.

A lot of trouble for just a dog? Maybe, but time invested in dogs and people when they're young pays off all their lives. And pups are pups only for a few months, while kids are kids for years. Besides, kids won't point and retrieve pheasants.

New home for an old boat

The limitations of my eight-foot dinghy for salmon fishing in deep water are too obvious to mention, so I decided to buy a bigger boat. But I didn't buy the boat I thought I would.

I called the numbers in the ads in the paper and drove around looking, but I didn't find what I thought I wanted.

One of the first boats I looked at was wood. The man who built it twenty-five years ago had obviously given it every bit of the care and attention a wooden boat needs. Neither motor was new, but both were in excellent condition. The trailer had several more years left in it.

I hadn't even considered a wooden boat. A wooden boat, especially that one, should belong to someone who could take the time to care for it the way the man who built it had. A wooden would only add to the demands on my time, so I kept looking.

Apparently a lot of people buy fiberglass boats because they can leave them out in the rain and sun and the hulls won't rot. I saw several sound hulls with mildewed canvas and corroded trim sitting on rusted skeletons of trailers. I wondered about the insides of the motors. Most of those fiberglass boats probably have owners with attitudes like mine: Buy fiberglass so you won't have to worry about it.

Some glass boats I looked at were in good condition. You can tell which ones they are by the prices. I was tempted to buy one of them, but by the time I added canvas, a second motor, and forward controls, I would have been near the price of a new boat.

Light & Dark

So I looked at new boats. To get what I wanted without compromise would have cost four times what I hoped to pay for something that would be simply good enough.

My mind kept going back to the old man and his wooden boat. He was selling it because he was too old to take it out anymore. I imagined how he must feel, how I would feel if I were he.

His boat would suit me perfectly. It was small enough for one person to launch and big enough for four people to ride in. The side-windows are the rear side-windows out of a Volkswagen Beetle and the windshield is from a '49 Ford, and it has a hand-crank windshield wiper. The new boat I looked at costing seven times as much didn't have a windshield wiper. There is a lot of character in that small boat.

I drove by to see if it was still there. It was, so I stopped and knocked on the door.

As I looked the boat over again, the man who built it and I discovered we have some things in common other than an affinity for boats with character. Although he is twice my age, we both prefer to hunt with bow and arrow and for the same reasons.

He first saw Port Angeles from the deck of a destroyer just after World War I and decided he'd live here someday. He moved here thirty-five years later. I wasn't much younger that he was when I decided the Olympic Peninsula was where I wanted to live, but it took me only fifteen years to make the move.

I told him I thought it must bother him, the thought of giving his boat into the hands of a stranger who might not take care of it the way he did. He smiled and said that was true.

While we were talking in his living room, a picture on his wall of a small town in some mountains caught my eye. It seemed familiar, but I didn't quite recognize it. I asked him where it was. He said it was a little mining town in Colorado. I said I knew that, but which one? Gold Hill, he said. He was born there. He showed me a picture of the house his father built there in 1901.

I told him I know Gold Hill. I grew up just a few miles from there, but half a century later. I was in Gold Hill a couple of weeks ago. Next time I'm back there, I'll find his house and take a new picture of it for him.

I hitched his boat to my truck and carefully drove home. There will be time in my life to take care of it. I'll make time.

Looking down on Christmas

East of the Northern Rockies, the land was covered with snow, silver-white in the moonlight. Looking down on Montana and South Dakota from 33,000 feet with an airplane load of packages behind me made me think, "This is what it would look like to Santa Claus."

Flying over most of America would not have made me think that. From high in the air at night, most of the country appears full. East of the High Plains, lights on the ground are an unbroken speckled blanket. No light is much beyond pistol shot of at least one other. It looks crowded, even in the farmlands of Iowa.

Not so in eastern Montana. Not so in the Dakotas.

The thin blanket of snow was bright enough, even in the waning moon, to make visible from six miles up, hills and creeks, highways and country roads, lakes and ponds. The lights of ranch houses appeared both cozy and solitary at the ends of dark threads of roads and mile-long driveways. Some are many miles from the nearest other lights.

Towns and villages are small and widely scattered. The small, snug clusters of lights look like the community centers they are. Billings is, by default, a big city.

To see Christmas lights from that height and distance requires imagination, but I've no shortage of that. I imagined what it must be like down there, to be a child caught up in the excitement of Christmas, excitement fed by home and family, by rural school and distant church, to go to bed on Christmas Eve and lie awake, waiting for morning, until finally the silence of the uncluttered landscape or a lullaby of windblown snow against the windows or a carillon of coyote calls brings sleep to a small, eager, hopeful heart.

Farther east, there is no distance, no space, no silence between lights. Sprawling cities merge with one another. They are too large to be community centers in the way that small towns far from other towns are.

Looking down and imagining, I see Christmas there more as one of strident ads yanking attention from one battery-powered or computer-driven technogift to another, a frantic season of crowded shopping malls open late for shopping convenience. I imagine cars fighting traffic and searching for parking in packed church lots where there is space aplenty except for Christmas Eve and one or two other holy days each year.

I imagine children going to bed the night before Christmas, ears faintly ringing from the last of the endless Christmas specials blaring from overloud big-screen color TVs. The music that lulls them to sleep is the low and steady rush of freeway traffic, a loud party across the street, an occasional medley of sirens.

I see the country Christmas tree as fresh cut, perhaps by the family whose living room it graces. Decorations are simple and varied, many of them homemade. The city tree is plastic or aluminum and the lights are all one color.

Neither image is that simple, that extreme, or necessarily true, but I am biased by my age, by my own distant childhood memories, and by my decided preference for wide open spaces over concrete canyons and close-packed condos.

Especially at Christmastime, I prefer to see life as Norman Rockwell paintings instead of as harsh images captured on tape and film that pour into our homes and minds, obscenities made marginally respectable only because we call them News.

I know there are happy people and healthy families in apartments in big cities. I know city kids love Christmas as much as country kids do. I know, too, that evil and degrading aspects of human life exist in the countryside as well as in cities. But sometimes it's good to put some knowledge aside and look at a world we'd like to see.

A perfect world has never been and never will be, but if we want symbols of what to strive for in our individual efforts to make the world better, we need look no farther than the hopes and dreams and joys of children as they drift off to peaceful sleep on the night before Christmas.

Suicide and sense of humor

My generation is not yet so gray-haired that my friends die of old age. And although flying is thought of as a dangerous profession, I can think of only two slight acquaintances who have been killed in airplanes.

A few school friends have died of disease over the years. Two were killed in car crashes and one in Vietnam. An uncle by marriage and a cousin's husband were murdered. My father's brother died of complications from a minor fall.

A faulty light at a swimming pool electrocuted the young son of some family friends. A friend of mine drowned trying to rescue a boy from a lake in Nevada. A man I knew in the service stayed with a runaway truck to steer it away from other traffic and died in the crash. But the thing that has killed more of my friends and acquaintances that disease or accident or murder is suicide.

Even if I don't count the high school friend who drank himself to death at forty-four, even if I don't count the heavy smoker who died of cancer at thirty-nine—even if I don't count them, suicide has killed the most.

The first one I was aware of was a childhood playmate, a bright social misfit who spent his adolescent years playing with chemicals and explosives. He shot himself one day when he was still in his teens.

The second was a friend I partied and drank beer with when we were of college age. I hadn't seen him for a year or so when I

learned that he'd parked his car at a police station an
shot himself.

The third was a doctor I knew only slightly, and only becau
my former wife and his wife were friends.

The fourth was a teenage boy I never met, but I knew his fath
when we were very young.   My parents and the boy
grandparents have been close friends for fifty years or so, but
include him in this list anyway because when the boy kille
himself, his father died of heart attack from the shock.

The fifth was a man who knew me because he was often one
my passengers when I flew for a local airline.   We'd buy ea
other a drink or a cup of coffee when we happened to run in
each other somewhere.   He seemed bright and outgoing, but I
killed himself.

None of those five were close friends. I didn't know any of the
well enough to know what was deep in their hearts and souls.

The sixth was a friend I worked with in a grocery store when I
was in his teens and I was not much older. He was memorab
for his brilliant sense of humor and his eager enjoyment of life.

His parents live just down the street from mine in Colorado, s
it was easy to keep in touch with him over the years when
visited my parents.   Somewhere along the line he becan
depressed, his mother told me later. And one night he drove in
a garage and left the engine running.

That one hit pretty hard. I found myself wishing I'd called
written more often so that maybe he might have been able to ta
to me, maybe give me a hint about whatever it was that wa
driving him to his death.   But I think now that I'd not hav
noticed anything out of the ordinary.

Because now one of my closest friends has killed herself. Aft
ten years of friendship, I had no idea she might do it.   Mayl
others did, others who saw her and talked to her more often tha
I did in the past couple of years. If I'd tried to make a list of
thousand people I knew who just might possibly sometim
consider, just consider, suicide, she, with her rich sense
humor, would not have been on that list.

I'd always assumed that a good sense of humor indicate
enjoyment of life and good mental health, but I'll never tru
sense of humor again. It's perhaps not just a line from a son
that people laugh to keep from crying.

Progress? Maybe not

The adoption of agriculture by humankind is generally considered the development that marked the end of tribalism and the beginning of modern culture. We accept that this was good, that it represents progress. Maybe not.

Prior to agriculture, human beings ran around in tribal groups probably less than a hundred people. They scrounged, scavenged, hunted, and fished for a living. They had nothing so substantial that they couldn't carry it when they moved to find plants or game or because someone located a dead mammoth in the next valley.

The amount of available food and the rate of travel to more food would have limited group size. One theory suggests modern sports teams tend to be close to a dozen members as a vestige of prehistoric hunting teams. A team of ten or twelve adult men would imply a like number of women the same age, several children, and a few old folks—around fifty to a hundred people.

While mortality may have been high because of lack of formal medicine to treat injury, populations would not have been large enough to foster infectious epidemics. And because the tribes were nomadic, they didn't live with accumulations of waste.

Then came agriculture. Whether people started farming for food or to make beer may be an open question, but the result is the same.

Agriculture requires hard work. It requires people to stay in one place while crops grow. That means permanent dwellings, storage facilities, and trade. That brought the evolution of cities Writing may have started to keep track of business transactions.

Agriculture made possible cities, written language, large an complex political and governmental structures, and the industria revolution. Agriculture was the first step toward technology i weapons, transportation, manufacturing, and medicine.

Cities required people to live in crowded groups with their wast and garbage. Transportation enabled societies to spread resultin diseases to other cities.

Better weapons allowed more destructive warfare. Manufactur ing gave more people means to earn a living, which made citie larger and more crowded and more prone to epidemic disease But advances in medicine eventually found ways to control c cure most diseases.

The adoption of agriculture sent us down the road toward all th perceived comforts and advantages of modern science and cultur we take for granted today. But in addition to music, art literature, cars, airplanes, computers, photography, transplan surgery, space travel, and television, we are afflicted with atomi weapons, modern warfare, overpopulation, smog, infectiou disease, gridlock, highway carnage, famine, pornography, organ ized crime, red tape, big governments, Moonies, hydroelectri dams, rap music, and television.

Those of us in modern countries work our tails off to pay for a the goodies in life and have little time or energy to enjoy them Those left behind in Third World countries are too busy trying t avoid mass starvation to join us, the privileged few.

As the rich few get richer and fewer, the poor many get angrie and more numerous. Those millions of us on top of the hea need worry more and more that the billions at the bottom ar going to get mad as hell and just not take it any more.

We are populated far beyond the point where utopian sharing c the wealth would do any good. If someone waved a magic want t give everyone on the planet an equal share in its wealth, we woul not all be equally wealthy; we would all be equally destitute There is simply not enough to go around.

There is no going back to that time before we rose at dawn t work in the fields until dusk. Except during vacations, of course when we head for the woods in small groups to live the simpl lives our prehistoric ancestors lived.

)ress for success

When I was learning to fly, my instructor wondered why I showed up in a coat and tie for my lessons. I told him that I 1ew I was a creature of imprecise, perhaps even slovenly, habits 1d thinking, and that I did not want those patterns to carry over to my flying.

Young people argue, as I once did, that we shouldn't judge ;ople on anything so superficial as clothing and hairstyle. On .e other side of the argument is the adage that clothing makes .e man.

Saints can dress like slobs, of course, and scoundrels can dress 1peccably. But that is beside the point.

How people make themselves look is a good indication of how ey feel. People who, given a choice, are content to look sloppy ·obably feel sloppy. People who prefer to look neat and sharp ·obably feel that way.

My father told me years ago, when we were arguing about what ithing was suitable for some forgotten occasion, that not only peoples' appearance *reflect* the way they view themselves, it *fluences* how they think and act. He said sloppy people tend to : sloppy thinkers, and people who look like ladies and ntlemen tend to act that way.

The argument was about my high school's dress code. (My iess is that public school students of today never heard the rm "dress code", but that supposition is based on limited servation.)

argued that what students wear to school is irrelevant. Dad gued that boys dressed in coats and ties and shiny shoes don't

31

scuffle and slap-fight in the halls the way those same boys do when they wear motorcycle boots, low-slung jeans, and unbuttoned shirts. He held that boys and girls treat each other with better manners and more respect when they are nicely dressed.

As with so many once-rejected bits of parental wisdom, I've come around to accepting Dad's views on appearance over the years.

I've been inside two courtrooms in two counties in the past few weeks. I wore a coat and tie when I went to court to explain the circumstances in which I got a speeding ticket. I got there a few minutes early and had time to look around.

Most of the two dozen people there were young, which probably isn't unusual for traffic court. The only skirt I saw was denim.

Nearly all of the young men wore jeans. The only two neckties visible in the place were on the judge and me. There was one jacket other than mine, that one worn over a sweater and perhaps a tie by another man about my age.

I didn't stay long enough to find out what that gentleman was charged with or how he fared before the judge, but my own fine was reduced substantially. Whether my appearance had any effect on the amount of my fine, I don't know, but I would be surprised if even the most objective judge isn't subtly swayed by the attitude of the miscreants facing him. And appearance reflects attitude.

In the other court, I appeared as a character witness for my daughter who pleaded guilty to her first traffic ticket. I wore a coat and tie. Katrina wore a conservative skirt and blouse. We tried to remember to say "Yes, your honor" and "No, your honor" instead of "yeah" and "unh-unh" as some of the others did. Maybe the way we dressed and addressed wasn't a factor in the amount the judge reduced the fine, but it certainly didn't hurt.

We didn't stick around to see how the next young defendant fared in his effort to explain why his ticket for driving eighty in a forty zone wasn't as bad as it looked. Leaning on the rail in faded denims and a sweatshirt while he made his pitch surely didn't do him any good, although a tailored suit wouldn't have gotten him off the hook on that one. On the other hand, if he'd been wearing a suit, maybe he wouldn't have been doing eighty in a forty zone.

One of those . . . what?

"Ah, my friend, you are one of those," the e-mail missive began. I could picture the writer looking down his nose at me, "one of those."

It started with an electronic chain letter asking only that I support refugee relief in Zaire and ask ten others to do the same.

Had the letter been conventional mail, I wouldn't have bothered to reply. But all I had to do was type a response and push a button. I said I thought such efforts futile, that it may be better to let a million die today than to have them and their millions of children die ten years from now. I signed off, "Sorry, but No," and gave it no further thought.

The response to my reply was written well enough that I didn't get mad when he accused me of having children, wearing leather, and eating fast food. My ire was not raised when he derided my smugness and called me a spiritual infant.

Had he been nasty, I'd have composed a biting reply that would have, with luck, been beyond his capability to comprehend. But, as he'd been civil, I was too:

Dear Peter,

You are too busy doing the kind of work my heart values (and my intellect considers ultimately futile) to spend a lot of time on this correspondence between us. I appreciate your taking time to respond and will try to keep this brief.

I was raised Unitarian in a politically and philosophically liberal home. I fervently support civil rights, not excluding the right to defend myself and others by any means necessary. I treasure the concept of individual freedom with commensurate responsibility that this nation was founded on.

"One of those"? One of what?

World population is doubling every couple of generations. doubt you are unaware of this.   Are you also aware that ii developed countries the population increase excluding immig ration is close to zero? And that the population increase by birth is greatest in the least developed (and least developable) parts o the world?

It is not that I don't care about individual human beings. It i: that I see us as a biological species subject to the same natura laws that control overpopulation in lemmings. Nature has way: of solving the problem, but they aren't pretty.

It is not just biology that limits populations. Psychology does it: part.

Any commodity in surplus is devalued. Any that is scarce i: prized. This is not just economics—it's human emotion.

Country folk tend to interact with strangers more than city folk Walk down the street in a town of two hundred and people wil smile and say hello as they pass. Try that in Manhattan. No only would people think you were weird, you'd get tired of makin; eye contact with strangers before you'd gone six blocks.

If the planet were a lifeboat that would support a limitec number of people, I would refuse to take on more than th number it would support. A few would live, the lucky ones, thos who were in the right place at the right time through no merit o their own. Others, just as deserving of life, just as good or bad a; those in the boat, would, through no fault of their own, perish.

You, I think, would pull everyone you could into the boat, ever though doing so would sink it and cause everyone to die.

Yours may be the morally superior position. If there is a Goc who values goodness and justice, He will surely smile upon you.

I know there is nothing fair about my taking the position that although I was lucky enough to be born in this rich country, or this lifeboat, I would deny others not so lucky a seat on this boat It's not fair, but life isn't fair. Biology isn't fair.

If it were possible for all people of every generation to have lif as comfortable as I have it, I would do what I could to help then have it.   But if trying to bring the starving billions up to my standard of living means dragging my grandchildren's down tc theirs, I say again, I'm sorry, but No.

Old school papers on a rainy day

One advantage of being disorganized is stumbling onto long-lost treasure while searching for something else. So it was when I opened a file drawer looking for daisy wheels for a seldom-used typewriter.

The wheels were under a thick folder of papers that I'd stuck in here when I discovered mice had been nibbling at it in the broom closet. My mother had given the folder to me when she was sorting her own files a few years ago. Old report cards or something.

The report cards were there, all right. So were other papers, a history of my educational development back to first grade.

In first grade, my otherwise straight-A record is marred by a B in arithmetic and the remark from Miss Shaw, "Eric does not care for numbers." Astute woman, that Miss Shaw. Didn't like 'em then and don't now, although, coming from a family firmly grounded in he physical sciences, I was forced to plug along at math until the intricacies of second-year algebra defeated me with finality in high school.

My mother saved programs from grade school and junior high "graduation" exercises, as well as childhood drawings and school papers. I forgot about daisy wheels and spent the next hour or so leafing through brittle paper and faded ink.

I have no idea where Mom got her hands on poems I wrote as a love-struck teenager. Merciful time had allowed me to forget the adolescent verse, but the memories of the girls are clear.

Light & Dark

How serious it all seemed at the time, though I laugh out loud now as I read a note added to the bottom of one ode to idyllic love and undying devotion: "I hereby void the feelings expressed in this poem. Jan. 4, 19—" The note was added not three weeks after I'd written the poem. I laughed again when I turned over the next sheet of paper and found another poem dated the same day as the note, a poem written for my newest true love.

My teachers didn't insist on dated papers before high school, so I can only guess my age at the time some tests, essays, book reports, and stories, were written. Style of paper would be a clue if I could only remember when we switched from Big Chief tablets to notebook paper, from pencil to pen, and from pen to typewriter.

Mom saved the handwritten bill-of-sale conveying my first bicycle from its previous owner to my father. It and my city bicycle license have been in that folder for thirty-eight years.

There are post cards with two-cent stamps and a four-cent stamp on a letter. There are Christmas cards made in Sunday school and pictures drawn with crayon.

There are several stories I wrote for school, all undated, of course. The oldest two are in pencil with just my first name at the top. "91 words" I wrote firmly at the bottom of one. I read the forgotten lines and the stories come back and I'm ten years old again. Or nine. Or maybe eleven.

There is a typed story with the grade B at the top and the teacher's note at the end: "A trite story, but done pretty well." That's very close to what an editor wrote when he rejected my first attempt at writing a novel. Thirty years separate the two notes. Maybe I'm a slow learner.

I got an A on my autobiography for sophomore English. Mom and Dad were pleased. "Of course it's an A," I remember telling them. "I got an A on it in seventh grade, and it's the same story so I just typed it up again for this year."

Necessity isn't the mother of invention. Laziness is.

I put the papers back in the folder more gently than I took them out. I should take better care of them, keep them away from mice and damp.

And I should also take better care of the box of my daughter's schoolwork that has been getting heavier over the years. I'll save it until she grows up and maybe has children of her own in school. Then some rainy day I'll give it to her.

Flag burning and Constitution

"I swing before your eyes as a bright gleam of color, a symbol of yourself, the pictured suggestion of that big thing which makes this nation. My stars and my stripes are your dream and your labors. They are bright with cheer, brilliant with courage, firm with faith, because you have made them so out of your hearts." This, said Franklin K. Lane, a member of President Wilson's cabinet, is the real meaning of Old Glory, the banner of the United States; for the flag is but a symbol of the nation. Whatever the flag to which you give allegiance, you are, in a very real sense, of its makers, as you are of the nation for which it stands.*

Compton's Encyclopedia, 1940.

Hats off!
Along the street there comes
A blare of bugles, a ruffle of drums,
A flash of colour beneath the sky:
Hats off!
The flag is passing by!

Henry Holcomb Bennett

To prohibit flag burning with a constitutional amendment is like smashing a fly on your nose with a hammer.
Burning a flag as an act of protest is a symbolic act. Destroying the multi-colored fabric of the flag is a trivial act and the result is no more consequential to the fate of the nation than is the

37

destruction of a handkerchief; it is monstrous and despicable only in its symbolism.

The flag is not the country. The flag is a symbol of what our country stands for. To most of us, it is a symbol of all that is good and admirable in the United States. We revere what it stands for. One of the things it stands for is the one thing that, above all others, makes our country great: the United States Constitution.

It is the meaning and spirit of the Constitution that gives life to our freedoms, not the parchment it is written on. And it is the traditions and concepts the flag represents that we value and respect. The flag itself is nothing but pretty cloth.

The Constitution concerns itself with great issues. It guarantees our basic freedoms, including what may be the most important freedom of all: freedom of speech. The Constitution does not and should not concern itself with flag etiquette and parking tickets.

Desecrating our flag by burning it, spitting on it, or trampling it into the mud, is a trivial act. Although it has enormous symbolic meaning, it should not be answered by force of law. To restrict freedom of speech even to the tiny degree that prohibiting the burning of flags would restrict it would be to cheapen the Constitution the flag stands for. Such a trivial amendment would desecrate the flag far beyond the efforts of some unhappy creature who can find no more eloquent way to express his dissent than burning a piece of cloth.

The trivial act of desecrating the flag, like a slap in the face, makes a huge symbolic impact. It should be answered by another trivial act that conveys great symbolic impact.

What more traditional American expression of heartfelt disagreement is there than a poke in the nose? It may cause a little pain and spill a little blood, but that is trivial compared to the message a fist to the nose conveys, not only to the recipient, but to all who see it and hear of it.

Trial by jury is a basic right we have, a right our flag symbolizes. Where law is sometimes blind and inflexible, juries of the people compensate for the law's rigidity. The law may say that a poke in the nose is assault and battery and deserving of punishment, but a jury of Americans would probably follow the precedent set by the Supreme Court: If a burning flag is symbolic free speech, so, perhaps, is a bleeding nose.

Parallel lives

I have a good friend from junior high school days who lives in a cabin in the woods in Maine. I hadn't seen him in a couple of years, so I went there for a visit last week.

In high school, Sandy and I read Steinbeck and Hemingway, and we knew we'd live in the woods like Thoreau and be famous writers someday.   We spent our spare time in the Colorado mountains hunting and fishing, hiking and camping. We sat in the back rows of the classes we had together and planned the next weekend's adventures.

We designed a still in geometry class and built it in his garage. We liberated grapes from his neighbor's vine that hung over a fence into the alley and made wine. Then we built a small fire in the garage under a coffee can, the old kind with a metal lid. We cooled the copper coil with snow and distilled our wine into brandy.

She still was slow, but it worked. Sandy and I were fifteen.

We got each other into and out of minor scrapes. When he couldn't get his '37 Dodge to turn over one cold morning, I advised him to build a small fire under the engine to warm the oil. But the fire I had in mind was smaller than the one he built.

The hood was open when the crankcase exploded.   Smoke billowed out of the alley. Sandy's hair was singed and his face was blackened. He found the dipstick in his front yard.

When I answered the phone, he shouted I'd tried to kill him and explained what had happened. I've never laughed harder, yet we remained friends.

Light & Dark

Once when we were exploring, I slipped on a rock face at the top of a cliff and slid toward certain death. With one hand, Sandy grabbed a tiny fir tree growing in a crack in the granite. He grabbed my hand with his other as I slid by. Had that twig broken, we would have died, but he didn't hesitate to save me.

After high school, Sandy went to college and I went into the Air Force. After college, he joined the Army and went to Germany. He stayed over there for several years teaching school, and when he came back to this country, he settled in Maine where he was born.

He bought twenty-five acres of woods with his savings and got married. At first, he and Linda lived in a tent. By the first Winter, they'd built a one-room cabin with a loft. They hauled water from a spring in buckets, cooked on a wood stove, and used candles and lanterns for light.

That was the way they were living when I first visited in 1980. When Barb and Katrina and I went there for a few days two years later, the cabin had become a log house. Three years later, it had electricity and a phone. Sandy and Linda built a quarter-mile driveway out to the road. Their daughter, Genevieve, was two.

Now they have a well and plumbing and a microwave oven. They still cook on the wood stove. They have no TV. They will always have no TV. They have no TV and are happy.

They've both worked hard these past several years. Sandy works five days a week and still makes time for his family and his writing. He writes adventure books for teen-agers.

My boyhood friend and I have independently found ways to live the way we talked about living thirty years ago. We both live in the woods, though at opposite ends of the country. We both had children later than most people do. We both write, although neither of us makes a living at it.

We both make our living flying airplanes, something neither of us seriously considered when we were young. We both learned to fly much later than most who make it a career. I fly across the country and Sandy runs a flying school that is growing steadily at a time when fewer and fewer people are bothering to learn to fly.

Neither of us has written the Great American Novel. Not yet, anyway. But one of us might. And if one of us does, we probably both will.

Disagreement kept civil

The young Boeing 727 captain and I have little in common. Matt is a tanned, handsome, Southern-California Republican. His philosophical beliefs are based in Christian theology. My view of human existence is more pragmatic than spiritual.

My belief that our planet is an overcrowded boat in danger of sinking allows me to look with favor on abortion. Matt believes that abortion is murder, period.

Although we agree that television is a major disaster for humankind, he believes the bloody amorality and its vacuous inanity of TV is forced on the public. I think TV is garbage because people prefer garbage. Sex and slaughter sells more beer and deodorant than serious discussion and drama.

Matt believes we are arrogant to think that we mere human beings, through science, can learn all there is to know about the universe. I think we are arrogant to assume that we mere human beings, animals that have been on this one tiny, insignificant planet for only an instant in universal history, are the creatures a god created the universe for in the first place.

To Matt, truth is absolute. He quoted Jefferson's, "We hold these truths to be self-evident..." to support his argument, equating "self-evident" with "absolute". I argued that truth is what people agree it is and quoted the same line back to him with emphasis on "We" and "these".

I almost never fly with Matt because I prefer routes with layovers in the Northwest and he prefers to fly to California, but last week, after my week of flying had ended in Cincinnati, I rode in his airplane to San Francisco in the dark hours of the morning. Usually I read or try to sleep in the cramped cockpit jumpseat, but Matt and I started talking and didn't stop.

41

Light & Dark

People who want to stay out of arguments avoid discussing politics and religion, but that's about all we talked about. Our deepest beliefs and strongest opinions seem incompatible, but we did not argue.

He asked if, since I favored abortion as population control, did I also favor war?

Historically, war has been ineffective as population control since the days when defeated peoples were routinely killed. War stimulates reproduction and birth rates go up. War tends to kill men, not women, and men are biologically expendable. Traffic accidents work better, I said. They tend to kill both sexes before they've finished breeding.

Matt listened to my answer with no more rancor than I'd felt when he'd asked earlier, "Why are there Democrats?"

He mentioned that he quit eating red meat a few years ago, for philosophical reasons.

So why is it okay to kill and eat chickens and fish but not okay to kill cows? I asked.

He didn't squirm or rationalize. He admitted the inconsistency troubles him, that it is a question he is working on but hasn't been able to resolve.

We could have talked for hours more if the flight hadn't come to an end, talked and disagreed without arguing. For in spite of our differences, we have one thing in common that transcends those differences: Neither of us insists that our ideas are absolutely right and that any conflicting ideas are beneath consideration. Neither of us hides behind dogma.

I didn't realize the greatest benefit of our debate until a day or so later.

When the holder of an opinion has arrived at that opinion after deep and careful thought, he assumes that anyone supporting any conflicting opinion has not given the matter much thought. Else why did he arrive at an opposite conclusions?

The real value in the discussion and debate between Matt and me is the renewed realization that two people can consider the same questions with equal care and intensity and arrive at different conclusions. That realization lends validity to opposing views and to the people who hold them. It makes us less quick to dismiss and condemn the beliefs and opinions of others.

a-a-CHOOOO!

've finally found confirmation of something I've always firmly
 believed despite the strong feelings of those who live and work
th me, not to mention innocent bystanders.

According to a medical note in no less an authority than
ader's Digest, the way I sneeze is the right way. I've never
red try to sneeze the polite way, the socially acceptable way.
n afraid that if I tried to suppress a sneeze, I'd blow my brains
t my ears.

t usually scares people when I sneeze. Sometimes it even
ares me. The recoil almost knocks me out of my chair. Once I
eezed in my sleep and woke myself up. So violent was my
eeze, it took the tidal waves in the waterbed several minutes to
bside.

My wife says that, when I finish sneezing, I mutter, "Damn."
ery time, she says. I didn't believe it, but I started listening.
d she's right. It's as involuntary as the sneeze. Most people
n't hear it, though. I say it quietly, and most ears are still
ging from the preceding sneeze.

Many things make me sneeze: pollen, dust, pepper, sunlight.
ldom do I sneeze only once. It's almost always three or four
es in quick succession with only enough time to refill my lungs
tween blasts.

o polite "achoo" when the sneeze center in my brain, or
erever it is, decides it's time to startle the neighborhood. First
mes the tickle in my nose, not a feeble sensation that can be
ored, but an insistent itch more on the order of large, excited
ts running around in my nostrils.

Then an involuntary sequence begins, a sequence that paralle
the series of electronic signals that launches an ICBM. My lung
fill, but not with a normal intake of air high in my chest. M
entire torso expands in an effort to inhale as much air a
possible, as if there is some internal contest to make each sneez
more colossal than any that has gone before.

When I'm outside in the yard or garden, no harm is done. Ar
ducks on the pond immediately take flight. If neighborhood dog
were barking, they stop. If they weren't, they start.

The chance of a series of sneezes in restaurants is high becaus
I use lots of pepper. Taking the top off the shaker and pourir
helps keep the stuff out of the air and out of my nose, put it isr
a perfect solution. Even when I have time to cover my face with
napkin or yank out my handkerchief in deference to others eatir
in the same building, the concussion is disruptive. No, the bla
doesn't blow plates off of tables and forks out of hands as it migl
appear. The startle reflex of the other diners causes that.

What's really exciting is when the cockpit is quiet in the midd
of the night at 35,000 feet. Lights are low, the radios are most
quiet, and the three of us are quietly thinking our thoughts whi
the autopilot flies the airplane. Good thing we wear our seatbel
all the time. No heart attacks so far, but a lot of people hate me.

A man I used to work with was extremely good at stifling h
sneezes. He grabbed his nose and pinched it shut while the pal
of the same hand held his chin clamped hard against his palat
The only sign he was sneezing was a facial twitch and streams
air whistling out through his eye sockets. He thought n
sneezing was barbaric. I told him he'd blow his eyeballs out c
the floor one day.

The June issue of *Reader's Digest* vindicates me: Sneezir
timidly may be hazardous to your health, it says. Holding you
breath, sealing your lips, or pinching your nose creates enormou
pressure to the nose and throat. Dr Raymond Wood says (don
read this right now if you're eating), "The pressure may forc
bacteria from your nose into your sinuses or into your ea
through the Eustachian tubes." Not to mention blowing you
brains and eyeballs out.

"The best thing to do," Dr Wood says, "is to cover your nose an
mouth with a tissue and go for it."

So there. WaaahhhCHOOO! Damn.

A hunt ends before the kill

thought I had several good reasons for not shooting the deer.

Only later did I begin to understand the real reason.

The only set of antlers I've seen this month appeared five inutes after the early muzzleloader season officially ended.

It took most of that Friday afternoon to pick my way along game ails through the grass and alder saplings from one end of the earcut to the other. Morning rain had left the ground soft, but I w no fresh prints. A stiff southwest breeze absorbed the unds of my slow passage.

saw no deer and no new tracks. Less than an hour remained fore the legal end of the hunting day.

The smart thing would have been to sit at the northwest corner the clearcut with the wind from my right and the light at my ck and hope that deer would move upwind from the woods to e grass just before quitting time. But I have trouble making yself sit still. I like to cover ground, even though I know sitting ill when game is likely to move works better. Besides, I'd heard at bridges on a nearby road had been removed since my last it to the area. I'd walk over and have a look, then come back d spent the last few minutes of the season searching the edges the clearcut with binoculars.

walked farther down the old road than I'd intended. When I t back to the clearcut, I hiked uphill to a vantage point and gan looking.

The deer was feeding into the wind less than a hundred yard
away. I watched until I was certain its antlers were not part
the brushy hill behind it, then I looked at my watch.

The season had been over for five minutes. The light was st
good, and five minutes is as close to correct time as most peop
keep their watches. I'd passed up legal shots in waning ligh
during previous seasons because cloudy skies made it dark
than the clock said it should be, so I could have rationalize
taking an extra five minutes on that bright evening.

The wind was gusty and I would have had to shoot standir
without a rest. But there were lulls, and the buck was in th
clear, broadside to me, and unaware that I was watching him.

Even if I'd shot him through the heart, he'd have been able
sprint into a briar patch that Bre'r Rabbit would have loved. F
the time I'd fought my way in and dragged the deer out, it wou
have been dark.

For all those reasons, I didn't shoot. I watched the buc
watched him snatch a bite of grass, then raise his head to loc
around, then sniff the air, move a step, and eat some more.
wondered how long it would take him to realize I was there.

Not long at all. After a minute or so, he saw me, froze for
second, and vanished like a wisp of smoke in the wind.

As I drove home, I was surprised to realize I did not fe
disappointment. I'd spent several days, walked many miles, ar
passed up my only available shot, yet whatever disappointment
felt was lost in the larger feeling of contentment. I felt prett
much the way I would have if the buck had been in the truck wit
my tag on its antler.

I thought about that for some time before it made sense to m
before I discovered the real reason I did not shoot, the reason
was easy to decide not to fudge five minutes, not to risk a wind
blown miss or a difficult retrieve.

The hunt, for me, does not end when game is in the bag, bu
just before. The point at which the option to kill is solely min
marks the end of a successful hunt.

The Spanish philosopher and hunter José Ortega y Gasse
wrote, "One kills in order to have hunted. One does not hunt i
order to kill."

The hunt is the thing. And because I chose to not kill that day
I look forward to the late season with eager anticipation.

Quit smoking? You bet my life

"Rush, when are you gonna quit smoking?" Forrest asked in a bar one afternoon in 1971. I'd started smoking when I was fifteen. Took it up to be one of the boys at the bowling alley where I set pins evenings and weekends.

People said it took twenty years to get lung cancer. I figured there'd be a cure before my two decades were up, but I was closing in on twenty years of smoking, and medical research was getting nowhere on a cancer cure.

I'd been thinking about quitting for a month or two. My wife didn't smoke, and pregnancy made her sensitive to strong odors. For the first time, I became acutely aware that my smoking bothered other people. I began to avoid smoking in the house. Smoking became inconvenient.

"When are you gonna quit smoking?" Forrest, a friend since early childhood, had asked as I lighted my fourth unfiltered Camel of the hour.

"I'll quit when the baby is born," I said. The idea had been forming for some time, to quit when my child was born, to give the baby a birthday present of clean air, to increase the odds that I might live long enough to see her grow to adulthood, to be more than a wheezing old man to my grandchildren.

But that was the first time I'd told anyone, the first time I'd committed myself to ending a most enjoyable addiction forever.

"Bullroar!" Forrest bellowed. "You'll never quit!"

"I'll bet you a thousand dollars I'll quit!" I answered with equal volume.

Light & Dark

The bar became quiet as heads swiveled to see who was ras
enough to bet a thousand dollars on anything.

We settled the terms: The first one to smoke any portion of
tobacco cigaret after the baby was born owes the other
thousand dollars. Anytime. For the rest of our lives.

At the time, it was a lot of money, but not an incomprehensib
one. We couldn't have taken a million bucks seriously, and
hundred would have been too low. During those first few days
either of us might have cheerfully paid a hundred dollars for
smoke.

Forrest would have an easier time of it than I would. While
smoked more than a pack a day, he smoked only a few hand
rolled cigarets.

I calculated my rate of consumption against the expected birt
date. I didn't want to be stuck with an unsmoked half-carton c
so. I smoked the last cigaret I'd ever smoke a few minutes befor
going into the delivery room to watch my daughter come into th
world.

Nightmares. For about a year, I had frequent nightmares. I
my dreams, I either forgot I didn't smoke and accidentally lit up
or I dreamed of getting caught sneaking a smoke. In either case
I'd wake up shaking in fear that I'd lost the bet and the money
Only after becoming certain that I'd been dreaming could I g
back to sleep.

Forrest had similar dreams with similar reactions. Even now,
sometimes wake up in the morning with a vague feeling of anxiet
that I can neither shake nor explain until I remember the dream
a dream of smoking a cigaret.

Because I started smoking young, I did not know what it felt lik
to be a healthy adult until a few months after I quit. But after th
first couple of weeks of coughing up the filth I'd been sucking int
my lungs, I began to experience a sensation similar to that c
watching *The Wizard of Oz* change from monochrome to color.

I began to smell fragrances that I'd not been aware of. A
previously unknown dimension of taste made eating a delight
And I could walk and run without gasping for oxygen. Bet aside
I can't imagine ever smoking again.

The tenth of November marks another year of healthy life for m
and another year of healthy life for my daughter.

Happy Birthday, Katrina, to both of us.

Their fish, my pleasure

The only thing as much fun as catching salmon is watching someone else catch salmon.

My brother, Jon, and his four-year-old son, Cassidy, visited us from Colorado last week. Jon lived in Seattle several years ago but never got a chance to fish for salmon. This was Cassidy's first exposure to salt water. On Sunday, after stops at Boulevard Herring for bait and at Swain's for licenses, Barb and I took them fishing.

We loaded lunch and fishing gear into our sailboat and motored out of John Wayne Marina. Cassidy began asking when we were going to start fishing before we cleared the breakwater. He didn't stop asking until we'd checked our crab pot in Sequim Bay and reached deep water in the Strait of Juan de Fuca more than an hour later.

The pot was crowded with crabs, four of which were legal-size males. Whether we caught fish or not, we had a seafood supper in the bag.

When the depthfinder indicated deep water, we throttled back and baited two lines with cut plug herring and stuck the rods into holders port and starboard. One rod had four ounces of lead and fifty feet of line out. The other had six ounces and a hundred feet. Cassidy wanted to know which rod was his. We told him his was the one he was sitting closest to. We trolled through a promising tide rip and waited patiently.

Well, three of us waited patiently.

"Yo, Uncle Eric. I'm not catching any fish."

49

His father and I explained that the catching of fish was out of our hands. Any complaints along that line would have to be directed to God.

Meanwhile, the four crabs were trying to get out of their kettle of seawater. Might as well fire up the stove and cook them while nothing was happening.

Murphy's Law as applied to fishing says, "If you want fish to strike, find something to do that takes both hands and all of you attention." Getting crabs ready for the pot was sufficient to proc Brother Murphy into action.

Two crabs were broken and cleaned when the shallow roc started bucking in the holder. "That one's yours, Jon," I said.

I dropped the crab halves I was rinsing and went aft to kill the motor. My brother took the rod out of the holder as the fish ran away with line. I helped him set the drag and sat back to do the fishing host's equivalent of backseat driving. I wish I'd had time to get out my camera to record the expression on Jon's face as his fish surged away, bowing the light rod. It's an unexpected sensation to inland anglers used to hatchery Rainbows and beaver pond Brook Trout.

The rod suddenly straightened. "I think he's off," Jon said.

"Maybe not," I said. "Crank fast and keep the rod up."

The fish was still on and was soon in the net, a nice, hooknose Coho, eight pounds and some on my tackle-box scale.

It was great. I had the excitement of vicariously catching the fish while my brother had the responsibility of cleaning his first salmon. Cassidy wanted to know when he was going to catch one.

When the same rod started jumping a few minutes later, we told the boy it was his fish. He accepted the change in his designated rod without a blink. Jon asked me to help Cassidy and went below for his camera.

The weight of the fish was more than small hands could crank against, so I had Cassidy help hold the rod while I reeled in line.

Barb netted the fish, another hooknose male, this one slightly larger than the first. My young nephew is a true fisherman. By the time he talked to his mother and sister on the phone that evening, his fish had grown to ten pounds.

Two fish were all we caught, but those two made the day perfect. The only thing as much fun as catching salmon is watching someone else catch salmon, and sometimes that is far, far better.

Baby feet and grown-up shoes

The reason I have trouble finding comfortable shoes is that my feet are normal and everyone else's are deformed.

Look at a baby's foot. It's nearly blunt. The toes form a nearly straight, angled line from big toe to little. Each toe is straight. The big toe forms a straight line from nail to heel.

Now look at your feet. Odds are the big toes are bent and touching the ones next to them. The little toes are likely curled and mashed into those adjacent.

Feet are the same shape as the shoes they spend most of their time crammed into. (We are, of course, appalled that the Chinese used to bind girls' feet to keep them from growing normally.)

When I was a child, my mother insisted that salesmen fit me with shoes that had plenty of toe room. Heaps of toe room. Room to grow into. Mom's motivation was stretching the budget, but her frugality allowed me to grow to adulthood with broad, straight, healthy feet.

People who built adobe dwellings high above the canyon floors of Mesa Verde hundreds of years ago cut ladders of shallow toeholds into sheer sandstone walls to reach their homes. I wondered, when I first saw them, how it was possible to get enough support with fingertips and a couple of toes to lift a human body to the next step. I figured out the answer the Summer I was sixteen.

Light & Dark

I wore no shoes that Summer. I'd been wearing shoes the previous year that looked better than they felt. The resulting cortisone shots in toe tendons were not pleasant. It became more comfortable to wear no shoes at all, and by late August, my toes were spread wide as an aborigine's, and my feet were tough.

Gravel became as comfortable as carpet. When my bicycle threw the chain on a steep hill, I put a bare foot down on the hot asphalt and braked to a stop. Those were feet that could have stuck all five toes into half-inch steps in near-vertical cliffs and climbed. (We, of course, consider barefoot peoples backward and unenlightened.)

I usually buy shoes a size too large and as wide as I can find. More than one pair of my tennis shoes—shoes that felt fine in the store—have holes cut in the sides for my big toes.

Normal shoes force toenails to curl under and ingrow. Tendons turning unnatural corners become inflamed. When forced into "normal" shoes, my feet can't carry me far without distress. Twenty miles becomes impossible.

I bought a pair of hunting boots last year. Ordered them plenty big and wide enough for two pair of socks. Unfortunately, they force my big toes out of their accustomed straight lines. My toes became numb after many miles up and down the hills. They didn't fully regain feeling for months.

I'd been getting away with wearing comfortable but unbeautiful shoes with my uniform for several years, but the airline recently dictated specific shoes that would be acceptable henceforth. I bought a famous, expensive brand. They're stylish, they're good looking, and they hurt like hell. I went back to my ugly shoes.

A solution is to stretch the torture chambers with shoetrees. The problem with that is, shoetrees are shaped to match shoes, not feet. I decided to make my own.

I spent a few hours cutting, carving, shaping, and sanding two slabs from a two-by-six to reshape my hunting boots. (To give you some idea of my problem, a two-by-four isn't wide enough.)

I hammered them into my boots, smeared the leather with grease, and hung them over the wood stove. I don't yet know if this will work. I'll give it a few days and try the boots on.

If it works, I'll whittle the trees down to fit my dress shoes. If it doesn't work, I'll bolt the shoetrees to broom handles and use them for oars.

Mom's funeral, as she planned it

One advantage of not dying young and unexpectedly is, you can plan your own funeral.

Mom was never one to leave details of her life to chance, so it was completely in character for her to have left none of the details of her death to chance or fate. Well, almost none.

Her file cabinets overflowed with the accumulated paperwork of her life: letters and legal documents, recipes and newspaper clippings, and extensive research of our family history back to the time of Cromwell. There was also a file marked Demise.

Mom planned thoroughly. She made it clear that she wanted to be cremated, but she left disposition of her ashes to us. My father, brother, sister, and I wanted a gravesite and a marking stone. We wanted to have a place to go from time to time, a place to sit and commune with memories. So we buried her ashes on a cold, sunny morning in a cemetery at the foot of the mountains in the town where she lived for the last half of her life.

Not in a modern burial park with flat stones flush with the ground to make mowing the grass easy, but a cemetery with granite and marble monuments standing upright among the trees, stones with names carved deep to keep them alive for centuries.

No one was there but family. We said a few words as the spirit moved us, each of us having a part in committing her remains to the earth.

In the months before she died, before her cancer put her in the hospital for the last time, my mother planned her service with the minister who would conduct it, a woman little more than half my mother's age, but one who knew and loved her and understood her spirit.

The service reflected my mother's Southern Baptist heritage and her humanistic beliefs. A quintet sang "Steal Away" and her favorite song, "No Man Is An Island". Although Mom was a feminist, she loved and respected tradition. If the quintet had bowed to feminist convention and changed the "man" in the song to "person", her ghost would have hounded them to eternity.

Readings from Psalms were balanced with readings that reflect humanist thought. She had selected poems by Edna St Vincent Millay and May Sarton.

My sister wrote a eulogy to our mother and read it during the service. It was more moving than any words someone not of our family could have written or spoken. I was never more proud of my sister than during those few minutes that she stood before friends and family, her voice strong and clear, and spoke of our love for our mother and of our mother's love for her family and for all humanity.

Mom wanted us to join the quintet in singing "Amazing Grace." She wanted us to sing it with gusto, so we did.

That song and the brief closing and benediction were a perfect closing of a family's and a community's formal farewell, but Mom's plans couldn't entirely preclude chance.

A woman I did not recognize stood just before we all would have risen to leave the church. She asked to say something.

I did not know her and had no idea what she might say, and for a few seconds, I was afraid she might spoil my mother's carefully planned service.

The woman explained that she hadn't seen my mother for several years since she'd stopped attending the same church, that she just happened to be driving by. From the overflowing parking lot, she concluded there must be a wedding, so she came inside to see whose it was. She hadn't known my mother was sick and didn't know that she was dead.

"I just had to stand up and say something," she said to us all. "Juanita Rush knows I always had to stand up in church and say something, and I didn't want to disappoint her."

I could imagine my mother laughing hard with the rest of us. She would not have been disappointed.

Future of hunting, if any

The more I read, the more pessimistic I become about the immediate future of hunting and fishing. The development of agriculture may prove to be the greatest misstep in the evolution of our species.

Agriculture made cities possible and necessary. Cities made the development of technology possible, if not inevitable. Agriculture supports far more people than does living off the land, and cities support far greater population densities than do field and forest.

Medical technology has overcome most of the diseases that living in one place for long periods of time brings. Modern medicine needed the stability of cities to develop; the cities needed modern medicine to defeat diseases that would otherwise become pandemic.

Now, with a world population of around five billion, we are facing famine. As more and more land is needed to grow food, less and less wildlife habitat will survive. What habitat remains will be in smaller and smaller pieces.

A given amount of land divided will not support the same numbers of species as that same amount of land as a unit. In ecology, it's known as the island effect. Wildlife habitat is being chopped into isolated islands by floods of humanity. Most species cannot survive in isolation. Hunting will become a luxury only the richest can afford until there is nowhere and nothing left to hunt.

Those who argue that the planet can feed far more people than now exist look to the sea for salvation. The potential for feeding humanity from the sea is unlimited, they say. But overfishing is already a problem. It was a problem even before the advent of drift nets. The sea is as finite as the land. Fish are no more infinite than were the bison and the passenger pigeon.

All this with the mere five billion of us crawling over this planet devouring the life on it and fouling it with our waste.

It has taken hundreds of thousands of years for us to reach five billion. The population will soon double. Double to ten billion in less than a hundred years.

Where will we live and what will we eat?

Animal populations are self-limiting. Grouse numbers grow for ten years and then crash to almost nothing before steadily increasing again. The mass migrations and drownings of lemmings are known to all of us since childhood.

Quail population densities tend to remain stable regardless of reasonable hunting pressure and other predation. When losses are high, brood size increases; when losses are low, quail lay fewer eggs.

When some internal mechanism for population control fails or does not exist, high population density enables diseases that would otherwise remain isolated to spread.

Classic population studies of laboratory rats read much like newspaper accounts of life in crowded cities. When rats are given all the food and nesting materials they need but are confined to a fixed space, the population increases into overcrowding. They have plenty to eat, but they don't have psychological elbow room. Rat family discipline breaks down, juvenile rats run in destructive gangs, infants die from lack of care, and rat society becomes chaotic.

Before human population doubles, starvation and unknown diseases will begin to cut humanity down to size. If medical and agricultural technologies are able to keep up with disease and famine, overcrowding will lead to wars far more destructive than any history has known.

Then, if humankind is lucky, what's left of us might crawl out of the ashes and start over. We'll be as we were eons ago, nomadic tribes of fruit eaters and root grubbers, scavenging what we can and learning once again to hunt and fish.

On elevators and turkeys

Watching people interact with elevators in a metropolitan hotel makes it difficult to defend the concept that human beings are more intelligent than turkeys.

Elevators have been around a long time. When they work right, they're terrific laborsaving devices.

Most modern elevators operate automatically. Those in the House of Representatives do not. We still pay people to sit on a little stool, open and close the doors, and say things like "Going up" and "Floor please." But, unlike most elevators, three in the House now sport twenty thousand dollars worth of new marble flooring. But I digress.

To summon a modern, automatic elevator, you push a button on the wall beside the door and wait. Eventually, the doors slide open. You may have to step aside to let people off before you step inside and push a numbered button corresponding to the floor you want to go to. You may have to step aside to let people off, but many people will not do that. They don't seem to understand that people have to get off a full elevator before others can get on. And that will bring me, in a moment, back to turkeys.

Elevator riding has evolved its own rituals and etiquette.

One never speaks to or looks at strangers. Riders stand well back from the door and face it. They don't face the walls or each other. No one smiles. No one looks into another's eyes. Neutral, bored facial expressions are required, and no matter how crowded the elevator, one occupant should not touch another.

The reason for ritually enforced avoidance of human contact seems to be the lack of space for psychological comfort. An elevator contains too many strangers for the enclosed space, even if they are only two.

Crowded cultures have traditions of highly ritualized procedures for human interaction. It's the same in elevators.

Most women prefer glass elevators that operate in an atrium, rather than conventional elevators enclosed in shafts. The reason is apparent. Human predators, most of them anyway, prefer not to operate in full view of the public.

Smoking on elevators is prohibited by convention as well as by law in most jurisdictions. The old rule that gentlemen remove their hats if ladies are present has largely fallen to common sense and sexual equality. Holding a hat invites having it crushed. Women don't remove their hats in elevators and never have.

To gain an understanding of how ingrained proper elevator behavior has become, try violating the rules sometime and watch what happens.

Step into a crowded elevator and stand just inside the door with your back to it and smile. Make eye contact with the other occupants, if they'll let you, and nod your head in greeting. You'll be regarded as a freak.

Or, if you are riding alone, stand facing the door with your nose an inch from it. The expressions on the faces of those standing inches from the other side waiting to get on are worth the ride.

Most elevator behavior rituals make sense when viewed as mechanisms for ensuring personal space. The one that doesn't is what makes me think of turkeys.

Turkeys are reputed to be so stupid that, if you put them on one side of a short length of fence and put food on the other side at the middle, the turkeys will stare at the food through the wire and starve rather than walk ten feet to go around the end.

When and elevator in a metropolitan hotel reaches the lobby and the doors open, a gaggle of people waiting to get on completely blocks the door. Those people can't get on the elevator until the riders get off, but they will not move out of the way.

Looking out from an elevator on that mass of uncomprehending faces, I know how those turkeys must look to the food.

Buddy: learning the game

Dog days are here again. Grouse season opened two weeks ago. I explained to my English Setter, Buddy, that the almon derby was more important that weekend. He pretended ot to understand, just to make me feel bad. So we went out late aturday afternoon for an hour. After all, opening day deserves t least token acknowledgment.

We drove to the closest patch of woods on a ridge near our ouse that is known to have grouse in it. At least it usually has. ut I was far more interested in watching my dog than in finding irds.

This is Buddy's third season. He's mellower at two-and-a-half nan he was last year. Two years ago, he was just a goofy puppy, appy to be running around in the woods and smelling delightful range smells. Last year, he was stone deaf most of the time. ouldn't hear either the whistle or my moderately raised voice. (I ever yell, of course.)

His hearing is much better this year. He hears the whistle most every time I blow it. He seems to understand, finally, that e are supposed to be a team, that I don't come along just to our him a bowl of water when he gets around to looking me up ery couple hours or so.

He not only stayed close opening day, he remembered to look ack now and then to see where I was. When he got out of sight nd his bell grew faint, one comeback whistle was enough to ring him in at a run. I began to wonder if I had someone else's og by mistake.

Light & Dark

We didn't find grouse, but at least we did the opening-da
honors. We didn't get out again until this week. We went to a
area in which grouse were thick five years ago, but which ha
been nearly barren more recently. Again Buddy acted the way th
training book said he should.

Even though we saw, heard, and smelled, no sign of grouse,
was pleased. Buddy was just tired. I tried to tell him that if he
start hunting at a reasonable pace instead of galloping in a
directions for the first half-hour, he wouldn't be tripping over h
tongue on the way back to the truck.

He recovered quickly, so we stopped on the way home at a plac
that usually holds several grouse. They don't fly far and the
tend to stay in the same small area filled with dense brush an
small trees. You can chase the same birds around all day. It
tough shooting, but the dog gets a good workout.

We didn't find grouse there this time. Maybe it was because of
logging operation just down the hill, or maybe it was the di
bikes yapping at each other's heels on the trail nearby. Or mayb
it was dry enough that the birds were still in the valleys to b
near water.

We went out the following day to a creek bottom that usuall
harbors a few birds and finally found grouse. That's grous
singular. One.

Buddy charged off like a greyhound out of the gate and slid to
stop in a solid point almost before he reached top speed. Th
commotion was more than the grouse could stand and
launched into a low orbit, maybe three feet off the groun
through the trees.

That clattering, low-flying bird was more than Buddy coul
stand still for, so he didn't. He broke the rules and gave chase.
couldn't shoot without killing my dog, although the ide
momentarily crossed my mind. I told him Whoa in a moderatel
raised voice. Told him once more and he stopped. Good thin
too. I don't think my vocal cords could have withstood anoth
moderately raised Whoa.

A toot on the whistle brought Buddy to me. His eyes told me h
knew he'd screwed up. I told him it was okay. Told him I knew
was easy to forget what to do on the first bird of the year. Tol
him that if I ever become good enough to hit every bird he find
then maybe I'll expect him to be perfect, too.

Death on a Saturday afternoon

might have gone salmon fishing that Saturday two weeks ago,
but I didn't. If I had, I doubt I would have checked the weather.
seldom check local forecasts anymore, perhaps too confident
at experience as a military weather observer years ago and
ore recent training in aviation weather makes it easy to judge
r myself what will come in the next day or two.   But I always
oked for wind warning flags on the tower above the Port Angeles
aterfront, those flags that don't fly anymore.
t takes me a couple of days to get back into the swing of
eeping nights after a week of all-night flying.   Usually, my first
uple of days at home are listlessly occupied by catching up on
e mail and local newspapers and puttering around the house.
ot even the prospect of a beautiful day of fishing can roust me
om home so soon after having been gone for several days.
thought of making an exception that Saturday.   The air was
ead calm in the trees as I sat down to breakfast. What I could
e of the sky was clear. It was too nice a day to waste indoors.
By the time I'd finished a second cup of coffee, the treetops were
aying gently. We began to consider spending the day sailing.
But Barb had things to do at home and I had errands to run in
wn, and by the time we'd discussed plans for the day, the wind
d become too strong for a pleasant sail.   Buy the time I got
me from town just after noon, the strait off Freshwater Bay was
ipped white. Glad I'm not out in that, I thought.

Light & Dark

Being preoccupied with errands and catching up on life a home, it didn't occur to me that the wind had come up s suddenly that dozens of boats, many larger than mine, might no have been able to get back to land before it was too late.

When I heard stories about that day on the water, thoughts o the trouble my ignorance of and accompanying lack of respect fo the sea might have cause me in recent years chilled my bones.

I thought of the calm, sunny days I'd spent fishing alone nea mid-strait in a small, open boat, ignorantly confident that I coul make shore if I started back the instant a hint of wind appeared.

I became ashamed of my smug belief in my own superior goo sense, symbolized by the fact that I always wear a life jacket whe on any water alone. Life jackets would have made no differenc to those caught in the cold, wet hell of that day. Good men wit far more water experience, wisdom, and good sense than I hav died in warm sun and cold water that day.

People on shore waited anxiously at the ramps as battered boat straggled in and the numbers of trailers dwindled.

I heard of two men who were picked up after their boat sli backward down the face of a wave and plunged stern first into th depths. I heard of another man whose outboard died over an over again from the force of being driven backwards down th faces of the breaking seas. Again and again he restarted hi motor and returned to the steering wheel amidships to hang o against the wind and motion. And when the metal spokes of th wheel snapped, he hung on to the hub, cutting his hands on th sharp remnants of spokes, steering his boat and hanging on t his life.

A methodical man, he always cleans the fish scales and bloo from his boat immediately after fishing. But he and his shredde hands let his boat wait overnight just that once. The blood tha day was his own.

That Saturday closed with diminishing winds, with fisherfolk snug in their homes and thinking back on the day in disbelie: That Saturday closed on empty boat ramps and vacant seas Darkness came down on a few empty trailers that would neve hold their boats again, and on a few cars and trucks that woul never again creak to the weight of their owners climbing ii to go fishing.

A monument to plumbing repair

I used to be a plumber, so I should have known better. Plumbing is fun. There are only three things you need to know to be a plumber: Sewage flows downhill, payday is Friday, and don't lick your fingers.

Yes, plumbing is fun. New-construction plumbing, that is.

It all goes together like Tinkertoys. A plumber walks through the skeletal frame of somebody's future home with a crayon and blueprints and draws fixture locations on the sub-floors and wall studs. Then he figures out the most efficient way to tie all the pipes together so that hot water comes out the hot faucets, cold out the cold, and the drains all run downhill.

After drilling holes, he cuts and glues the black plastic waste pipes and fastens them in place. Then he cuts and solders the shiny copper supply pipes and fastens them in place. Then he puts air pressure in the copper and water in the plastic so the inspector can check for leaks. He makes one last check to be sure he hasn't got hot water piped to the toilet supply (very embarrassing), loads up his tools, and goes home.

There is one other nice thing about plumbing a new building: It's easy to temporarily remove a few wall studs to get tubs and showers into the bathrooms.

Plumbers hate repair work. No matter how simple a job looks, if it looks like an hour will be enough, it'll take half a day.

In old plumbing, fixing one leak starts another. What appears to be simply a worn washer turns out to be a cracked faucet. Twisting off the ancient faucet loosens a joint back under the

house where the crawl space is so low, the rats drag their bellies
and by the time you move enough musty dirt and push through
fifty years' accumulation of spider webs, the leak has created
hog wallow. Yep, plumbers hate repair work.

So I should have known better than to replace the built-in
shower in our doublewide mobile home.

I'd been putting it off from the day we moved in several year
ago. What the heck, so it's cracked around the drain. Epoxy i
ugly, but it holds. So what if the drain is the highest point in th
shower and stands like a low atoll above a shallow sea.

One reason I avoided the job is the difficulty of getting a thirty
two-inch shower through a twenty-six-inch door. But I took th
old one out in fragments and put in a new two-piece, one o
which you bolt the wall section to the base after you get bot
pieces into the bathroom. Piece of cake. I figured maybe fou
hours for the job if all went well, a little longer with the inevitabl
complications.

Once the old shower was out, I saw why it had cracked. Th
jerks who built the mobile home ran the drainpipe through a jois
next to the drain. A minor leak years ago had caused the particl
board sub-floor to swell a little and raise the center of the shower
The drainpipe and trap, imprisoned in the joist, stayed put
Naturally, the shower cracked, which made the leak worse, whic
made the sub-floor swell more, which raised the center of th
shower more and created a potential fish farm.

It was a typical plumbing repair. Murphy the Lawgiver was
plumber.

I asked myself how I could have possibly been so stupid as t
think there was the remotest chance in hell I could remove an
replace a shower in four hours. Then, after a time of therapeuti
wailing and gnashing of teeth, I crawled through the spider web
under the house and went to work.

Now, four days later, it's all done. All except for a bit of shee
rock, paint, and trim. A big new drain runs straight to the sewe
pipe. The floor under the new shower is level again, and th
water all runs downhill.

I don't know what the life expectancy of a modern mobile hom
is, but that shower will outlast it. Future archaeologists will find
it standing alone in the woods, straight and level, with rainwate
gurgling unimpeded through the drain.

Running out of room

wonder where they think they're going to put everybody.
I wonder if doctors who wipe out disease, if humanitarians who strive to feed starving nations, and if moralists who fight birth control and abortion have given any thought to the future beyond their own lifetimes.

Population projectionists say there will be twice as many of us in another generation or so, maybe ten billion people. That is more than three times the planet's population when I got out of high school, and much of the world was overcrowded even then. Most of the increase will be in the poorest countries, those least able to feed themselves, much less billions more.

When I was in grade school, the idea of running out of food was preposterous. Not only was much of Earth still uncultivated, we'd hardly begun to tap the limitless resources of the sea.

Today we know that irrigation carries so much salt to the land that, in time, it becomes sterile. The Sumerians were the first culture based on irrigated agriculture. Archaeological evidence indicates the variety of the crops they grew became narrower with time, those least tolerant of salt disappearing first, the most tolerant, last. Then the Sumerians disappeared.

Today, especially here in the Northwest, we're finding out how limited a food resource the oceans really are.

Jeremy Rifkin, in his article "Beyond Beef" in the March/April 1992 issue of *Utne Reader*, argues, as others do, that the grain we feed to cattle in this country alone would feed four hundred million people. Worldwide, the grain fed to cattle could feed billion.

That's a very nice idea, feeding people instead of cows. Nice fo today, that is. But what are the billions of offspring from th billion we feed today going to eat in the next generation? An what happens to all of us in the world if all the food is efficientl distributed so that nobody starves and all the food is consume every year? What will happen the first year crops fail?

Even if everyone in the world agreed today that reducing th planet's population is necessary, even if everyone in the worl were issued lifetime supplies of contraceptive devices at ag twelve, even if morning-after abortion pills were two-for-a-penn in vending machines, even if the Pope came out for birth contro the population would continue to climb. And since every yea sees another disease or two controlled, the number of survivor will increase.

If the poor and barefoot peoples of Earth were not poor an barefoot, the drain on food, materials, and energy—and th resulting pollution—would make life impossible for everyone.

Nature is good at controlling populations. When there gets to b too may of something, they either die of epidemic disease o starvation.

Some animals control their own populations by adjusting thei rate of propagation to the population density, but the humar animal does not. And we have managed to control most disease that flourish in overcrowded conditions. Most, but not all.

Cholera is making a comeback in some parts of the world. S are a new form of tuberculosis and a drug-resistant strain o malaria. The impact of slow-growing AIDS is just beginning t make us aware of the effect it will have on much of the world' population.

"One of the axioms of viral epidemiology is that when th population of a host...increases, the chance of a disastrou epidemic also increases," says David H Freedman in *Discove* magazine in February 1992.

The ultimate retreat from the problem of too many people on to small a planet is the conviction that God will provide a solution.

It's hard to disagree with that. If we don't solve the populatior problem soon, God or nature certainly will.

But it will be ugly.

Booklist education

Ten years ago, I calculated that, at what I guessed was a reading rate of one hundred books a year, I'd be able to read only another four thousand or so in my lifetime. Because most of whatever education I have acquired comes from reading, not from classrooms, I was dismayed.

It turns out I was optimistic. I've kept track of the books I've read in the past two years. I read only sixty-six books in 1990 and sixty-five in 1991. That's only two thousand books between now and my eightieth birthday. And when I consider that every twentieth book or so is one I've read before...

I started keeping a book list in my computer after reading Louis L'Amour's memoir, *Education of a Wandering Man*. L'Amour, the late prolific writer of western novels, kept annual lists of the books and plays he read as he worked his way around the world beginning when he was a boy. His list for 1930 numbers one hundred and fifteen. He was twenty-two years old.

L'Amour's 1930 list, at an age at which I was barely out of comic books, runs heavily to philosophy and the plays of Eugene O'Neill. Only five of the total are works I also have read.

My own lists pale in both quantity and quality, although my book count would be higher if it weren't for the two or three dozen magazines and seventy-five newspapers I read each month.

Fiction comprises the bulk of my reading, although there is respectable representation of history, biography, and the occasional classic.

L'Amour read one hundred and twenty works in 1931 and again the following year. But in 1932, he lightened up. In addition to most of Shakespeare, he read ten volumes of *The World's Best 100 Detective Stories*. He rested his eyes in 1935; his list numbers only seventy-three.

Louis L'Amour had little patience with people who claim to have no time to read: "In the one year during which I kept that kind of record, I read twenty-five books while waiting for people."

That made me feel less apologetic about taking a book with me wherever I go, often to the embarrassment of my family.

L'Amour got his education from the life he led and the books he read: "The idea of education has been so tied to schools, universities, and professors, that many assume there is no other way, but education is available to anyone within reach of a library, a post office, or even a newsstand."

This self-educated novelist knew things our political leaders should have known: "During the Vietnam War era, people were led into all sorts of foolishness by simple ignorance of a part of the world strange to them. Many believed that North and South Vietnam were one country divided, but such was never the case except briefly under French administration."

His memoir is sprinkled with such gems as, "The sale of poetry books goes up during most wars," and "Adventure is nothing but a romantic name for trouble."

For perspective, it would be hard to beat L'Amour's observation that, "We view the devastation of Hiroshima with horror, but such things happened regularly in the ancient world." And for a different view of modern America, ponder this: "I have never found a society that was not materialistic. If you find one, you may be sure it will be dying."

Not a bad education for someone whose school had no walls.

I have friends who live in the Maine woods. Jenny, age nine, reads constantly. And she's been bumped up a grade in school and takes science courses in a grade level above even that.

Her teacher mentioned to her parents, as much in wonder as in complaint, that Jenny reads all the time in class, even when she should be doing other things. I'll bet that few teachers of modern children can say that about a student.

I'd like to read Jenny's book lists twenty years from now. That young girl in her log cabin in Maine is getting an education her bored, TV-watching peers will not, and she's getting it not so much because of school as in spite of it.

Overkill on gun control

The idea was to raise the group's consciousness, but I'm afraid all I managed to raise was its blood pressure. Giving a talk against gun control before a Unitarian-Universalist church group is a bit like arguing the virtues of vegetarian diet before a cattlemen's convention.

Roots of the Unitarian-Universalist Association's profound liberal tradition are old and deep. Most members are strongly, even fiercely, liberal in personal and political outlook. Given my subject and my audience, I felt like a mouse at a cat convention.

Knowing almost everything I had to say would be resisted by almost everyone, I found myself trying to write a jury summation rather than an informal talk. I wanted to make logic and evidence supporting my position irrefutable when what the occasion demanded was a stimulus to thoughtful discussion.

When I accepted the invitation to speak, I wondered how I'd fill forty-five minutes. After I'd gathered references and started outlining, I wondered how I could keep it under four hours.

Since I didn't have time to try to make an airtight case, I tried to outline the biological and cultural evolution of the concept of self-defense, the legal and historical evolution of weaponry as it relates to self-defense, and the discussion of the right to keep and bear arms and its relationship to the militia codified in the Second Amendment. An outline unadorned is boring, so I fleshed it out with quotations from the founding fathers and Supreme Court decisions and with anecdotes of recent uses and abuses of firearms. I tried to get my listeners involved and to keep to a minimum statistics on declining accident rates and the instances of legal and proper uses of firearms in self-defense.

Light & Dark

A brief discussion period revealed deep fears and strong beliefs of those who don't accept my conclusions.

Although I'd tried to show that, historically, moderate and reasonable gun controls almost always evolve toward severe and unreasonable controls, people asked why people object to reasonable controls such as gun registration. "After all, we register cars."

I don't think fast enough on my feet. I should have pointed out that we register cars, not to save lives but to raise revenue, and that registered cars kill thousands more people each year than do unregistered guns.

When someone mentioned the Vancouver-Seattle comparison published in *New England Journal of Medicine* in 1988 showing a much higher murder rate in Seattle where handguns are common than in Vancouver, a city the study deemed otherwise comparable to Seattle, I should have remembered the politically-incorrect figures from that same study that point out that Seattle has a larger underclass than Vancouver. The murder rate among Vancouver whites is slightly higher than the rate among Seattle whites, but that the homicide rate among Seattle's black population is six times and the Hispanic rate is more than four times that of Seattle's white population.

But maybe it's just as well I stayed away from the statistics of crime related to culture. These days, it's probably impossible to discuss such things, no matter how factually, no matter how objectively, no matter how carefully. Cultural lines are often almost the same as racial lines, and anyone willing to discuss cultural aspects of crime risks being branded a racist. It's convenient; if we can label an argument "racist", we don't have to consider it anymore.

Perhaps a few eyes were opened, although perhaps not by me. More than one gray-haired member of the congregation mentioned owning guns and sometimes carrying concealed pistols. The startled reactions of the others to such revelations will prompt more thoughtful re-evaluation than will anything I said.

Give the liberal church group credit for this: They invited me to present ideas to them that they knew they would neither like nor agree with. That's the same as a conservative, pro-life congregation inviting an abortionist to speak. Imagine that, if you can.

70

Who nose?

The sight of people running around wearing rings and studs in their noses raises a delicate question I have so far resisted the impulse to ask. Besides, it's none of my business. But the growing fashion trend over the past few years of poking permanent holes in various parts of bodies to hang doodads and gewgaws from raises the question of motivation.

Tattoos have, until recently, been sported more by the lower social and economic classes, especially military men and primitive tribes, than by better educated and more intellectual members of modern societies.

The tattooed percentage of the American prison population is much higher than that of those of us outside the walls. That might be because it's more difficult to identify an average-looking robber with a bland face than it is to identify one with a tattoo on his forehead. But it's more likely that someone who can't see far enough into the future to realize he might not want a cobra wrapped around a bloody dagger on his arm all his life probably can't project far enough into the future to see that if he robs a bank this year, he will likely be in prison next year.

A generation ago, young men in military service hit the tattoo parlors the first chance they got after basic training, usually after a few hours in a bar. Late one Saturday, when I was stationed at an air force base in Illinois, a bunch of the boys came back to the barracks after a night on the town. They all had bright new tattoos on their arms. All but one had the usual themes: flags, hearts, and the like. All except a small, quiet, bespectacled boy who hadn't really wanted a tattoo, but had gone along with the crowd. He had, and no doubt has to this day, a cute little cartoon-style skunk on his forearm. His nickname from that day on, although we all liked him, was Stinky.

Some tattoos are considered works of art, although most of us prefer to hang art on walls impermanently. Other tattoos, often self-inflicted in reform schools, are crude brands signifying gang affiliation.

Sailors in the days of sail are said to have worn their meager wealth in their ear lobes to avoid losing it. I'm not sure why American men presumably beyond adolescence started wearing tiny little ear studs. Must be a fashion statement.

Younger people, those of the purple Mohawk crowd, sometimes have enough rings and things in their ears to start a hardware store. If that's a fashion statement, I guess I'm not listening.

Modern people brand and tattoo livestock for identification. We put rings through the septums of cattle to make it easy to lead them around and chain them in their stalls. From that comes our image of someone leading his or her spouse by the nose, an image implying complete control. Now, after a couple of decades of women's liberation, some young women wear rings in their noses. (I'm not going any further with that because my mailbox isn't big enough to hold all my bills and hate mail too.)

Primitive tribes scar and tattoo themselves. Some bore holes in their ears and lips and insert progressively larger plugs to enlarge the holes. Some wear bones in their noses. Makes you wonder where the expression, "I've got a bone to pick with you," comes from.

Caged animals and people mutilate themselves, maybe out of boredom. Mental cases bang their heads on walls and tear at their own skin.

Maybe permanent pictures painfully applied to one's hide are works of art, expressions of self, or fashionable decoration. Maybe multiple ear rings and pierced noses are modern fashion fads and not a reflection of discomfort with modern life and an urge to return to a primitive state.

I wonder about these questions now and then, but what I really want to know about people wearing bejeweled studs in their nostrils is, exactly how do they manage to pick their noses?

The lamp and the golden door

"Give me your tired, your poor, Your huddled masses yearning to be free..."

The Statue of Liberty has been welcoming immigrants to this country for more than one hundred years. Disagreeable as it may be to our national self-concept, it may be time to become less generous.

Whether immigration is good or bad depends on point of view. Surviving American Indians no doubt view it differently from second-generation European Americans.

Unlike most subsequent immigrants, we newcomers did not adopt the ways of those who were here before us. When our new culture clashed with the old, we practiced ethnic cleansing of a most brutal, deceitful, and unchristian sort until our hosts were almost eradicated as peoples and as cultures.

Once we Europeans arrived, we invited all our friends. "Come on over! Great place, this America! Plenty of everything for everybody, once we get rid of the savages, of course."

The New World succumbed to the will of immigrants from the Old. North America became the goal for those whose lives were unpleasant elsewhere. And for over two centuries, we have opened our hearts and our country to immigrants.

Not all newcomers are equally welcome. We've always shown preference for those most like ourselves—white, Protestant, Anglo-Saxon—but we've made big-hearted exceptions for others such as the Irish Catholics and the Chinese whenever there were canals to be dug or railroads to be built.

Light & Dark

Except for those Africans who came here in chains, America wa
preferable to the old countries, even for those who had to endur
prejudice and indignities when they arrived. Those were sma
prices to pay for one of the greatest of human desires
opportunity.

Immigrants traditionally have worked hard to becom
Americans. They have instilled in their children the belief that, i
this rich land, they have no excuse for failure. All you have to d
is work hard and be a good citizen.

For a long time, that was literally true. Perhaps it still is, bu
that message hasn't gotten through to hundreds of thousands c
American-born who waste their lives in the streets and alleys c
our cities, seemingly without hope, without ambition, withou
goals.

The message may be a joke to those who lose their farms o
businesses or jobs to economic and political forces most of u
can't understand and who discover they can't all simply start ove
at the bottom and work their way back up.

We, as a nation, have always had plenty of room for everyone
Now we do not, but we haven't yet recognized or admitted it.

North America is still a better place to live than most other part
of the world. And, even though it becomes less desirable as i
becomes more crowded and as its resources dwindle, it wi
continue to be better than places where life is without food
without hope, and without opportunity to make life better.

As the world becomes more overpopulated, more and large
parts of it will be supporting people at the edge of existence, suc
as Somalia, places in which a slight disturbance in politics o
weather can push entire populations into starvation.

As political divisions become more fragmented as in Yugoslavi
and the Soviet Disunion, internecine fighting will produce mor
refugees, which will stress struggling political structures eve
further, which will lead to greater and more widespread chaos.

More and more people throughout the world will becom
refugees. They will try to come to North America, the last hig
ground in an inexorable flood.

The question is, at what point should we, will we, and can w
decide we cannot continue to accept the world's huddled masse
of tired and poor because we have too many of our own?

On cops playing cowboys

Tragic as the deaths in the attack on the cult compound in Waco, Texas, last week may be, and tragic as the deaths in the siege of the Weaver family in Idaho last year may have been, the conduct of government forces involved made those bad situations worse than they had to be.

Police raids that have become common in our holy war on drugs seem to have set a style for raids and searches in other matters. We see drug dealers as low life forms, not citizens like the rest of us, so we don't get upset when police smash down house doors, verbally and physically abuse the occupants, destroy furniture, smash beds, bash holes in walls, and confiscate everything of value, some of which never gets to the evidence lockers and is never returned. After all, it's only drug dealers.

But often the victims of these raids are innocent. Sometimes raiders are at wrong addresses and the people being shoved around, cursed, and frightened beyond imagining are people like you and me, people like your parents and mine.

Innocent people may be more likely to resist sudden, unannounced, violent raids on their homes with force of arms than criminals are. Innocent people don't expect the good guys to attack them. Criminals do expect it. They know the rules. They usually surrender, get out on bail, and go home. It's all part of the routine of being a criminal.

In Snohomish County, police acting on a false tip smash into a home expecting to arrest bank robbers and murderers. A young mother instinctively moves to protect her children and a policeman shoots her to death.

Light & Dark

In California, a man just home from the hospital after catara
surgery hears someone break into his house. He grabs his pist
and goes to investigate. It's police officers with a search warrar
They kill the innocent homeowner. No contraband is found.

In Oklahoma, a tipster reports that a man has an illeg
machine gun in his large and valuable firearms collection. Agen
from the Bureau of Alcohol, Tobacco, and Firearms watch tl
house and observe the man for several days. Then, when he
away from his home, the BATF agents smash down the fro
door, trash the house, destroy gun cabinets, scatter firearn
around on the floor, and find nothing illegal. They walk o
through the hole in the house and go away.

Had the police agencies involved in the Snohomish County ra
watched the house long enough to notice there were women a
children inside, they might have elected to apprehend the m
they thought they wanted as they went about their busine
outside. That wouldn't have been as exciting and wouldn't ha
made dramatic news video, but it wouldn't have killed a
innocent woman, either.

Had the California policemen approached the subject of the
suspicions on the sidewalk, identified themselves, and serv
their warrant, they could have peacefully conducted a sear
without killing a half-blind old man.

And had the BATF agents in Oklahoma done the same, th
could have used the keys to the front door and to the gu
cabinets in their search for the non-existent machine gun, b
that wouldn't have been as much fun.

Police agencies should stop playing cowboys and Indians. Th
should watch less television and read more history. Front
assaults against modern firearms get lots of people killed. We'
known that since the Civil War.

The most asinine statement to come out of the standoff at Wa
so far is that of BATF representative Sharon Wheeler: "The pro
lem we had was we were outgunned. They had bigger firearn
than we had." And she said they were also concerned abo
women and children! So what could they have done with bigg
weapons?

The government agents weren't outgunned in Texas. Th
defeated themselves with silly, B-movie heroics.

'aking care of a good old dog

Vhat do you do with such a dog? Not Buddy, my bright, generally well-mannered English Setter, the friend and nting partner I've had and trained since he was a few weeks I. Our other dog.

tephanie was half-grown and already named when we got her. e was, or is, our daughter's dog, mostly black Labrador. As en happens with children's pets, the dog stayed home when r person moved away and married.

n the context of working dogs, she's not good for much of ything. She's not inclined to retrieve. We don't know how she s treated before she came to live with us nearly a decade ago, t she cowers from the motion of throwing a ball or Frisbee as if pecting a blow.

ireworks drive her insane with fear. A year ago when we were ay from home on Independence Day, fireworks two miles away d out of her sight drove her to break a hole through her wire nnel and claw the paint and weather stripping from our front or in her craving for escape from whatever demons the pops d bangs evoked.

tephanie is so fearful of the world, she will not walk ahead of a n. She'll force her way past my legs in a narrow path of llway to escape the burden of having to lead the way. She erts herself only when the object is food, forcing my dog away m the choicest tidbits as they lick clean our dinner dishes.

ler greatest pleasure in life, other than cleaning plates, is going walks with Barb in the mornings or after work and finding foul ngs to eat along the road. What do you do with such a dog?

'e replaced the fence-wire kennels with stakes and chains soon er Stephanie broke through the wire. The next thing she did s go over a fence at the back of our lot one night, probably to investigate some rodent in the brush beyond. Her chain was lon enough that she could reach the ground on the other side withou hanging herself. She even managed to climb back to our side the fence, but she ripped a gash in hip and groin on barbed wii at the top.

In spite of one of those plastic cones around her neck, sh promptly pulled most of her stitches. The vet said it would hea in time, without the stitches. But the dog wouldn't leave th wound alone, and, although most of it closed, her constar licking kept it from healing completely. But her body kept tryin, and scar tissue kept growing.

Our regular vet looked at it when the dogs were in for the annual shots. He recommended we have the mass of growth cu off and sent to a lab for analysis. We agreed, but explained we have to come up with a way to make her leave the incision alor or we were wasting our time.

Stainless steel stitches with half-inch ends like barbed wii should have discouraged her, but they didn't. She tore out thre the first night. I took her back to the vet and he stapled the ga shut, double-wrapped her leg, and sprayed on something that supposed to taste so bad the dogs will leave it alone. I als bought a plastic muzzle to keep her from licking and gnawing the bandage and stitches.

The muzzle was a mistake. She used it to push the bandag down and scrape the wire stitches out. By then, there wasn enough intact skin to stitch again.

I entertained the idea of having the vet put her out of my miser but only for a moment. My daughter's, and now my wife's, do may not be my favorite member of the family, but she is famil Even I would miss her.

She's not happy right now. I cut the middle section out of five-gallon plastic bucket and bolted it onto the plastic cone. St can't eat or drink with the rig on and, restricted to tunnel visio she crashes into things. But she can't even see her wound, muc less nibble at it. The bucket on her head may be her last chanc for survival.

So what do you do with such a dog? Pets are not toys to t played with today and discarded tomorrow. Pets are membe our families. They are dependent on us for everything.

What you do with such a dog is everything you can.

Deciding whether to carry a gun

A friend of mine came up against modern reality Easter weekend and it scared him. He is a former Marine in superb physical shape. Although he is an expert on firearms, has an extensive gun collection, and is a member of the NRA, he doesn't carry a pistol and does not have a permit to do so. Not yet.

He and his wife parked in front of a convenience store near SeaTac airport on Sunday night and walked in on a tense scene. There were four people already in the store, an unhappy looking clerk and three young men.

What caused the tension was not that the three men were black, it was that one stood near the front windows looking outside frequently. Another stood around doing nothing much while the third tried to engage my friend in casual conversation at the counter.

It occurred to my friend that he and his wife had walked in on a robbery in the making, that their presence was keeping the three from holding up the clerk. It also occurred to him that they might themselves become victims of urban wealth redistribution.

He spied a copy of *Women & Guns* on the magazine rack and asked his wife if she'd seen that issue yet. She picked up on the ruse without hesitation and said she had it already.

That gambit appeared to give the three men momentary pause, but they followed the couple into the parking lot. My friend opened the door for his wife and closed it after she got in. As he walked around to the driver's side, he wondered if they were going to be robbed and maybe killed or if he were over-reacting to stereotype. And part of him was wondering if he could take all three if he had to, they being young and perhaps armed while he was neither. The talkative one met him at the car door trying again to begin a conversation. One of the three hung back a little on the passenger side and the third moved to the rear of the car.

Apparently noting the upright bearing of my friend, the talkative one asked if he were in the military. He said he was. His wife meanwhile, sitting in the car, slipped her hand inside her purse making sure the man on her side of the car could see her do it.

The talkative one still seemed eager to press on, the one at the rear of the car was, perhaps, indifferent, and the third tried to signal the other two that he didn't think the enterprise was a good idea. He prevailed, and my friend and his wife drove away.

His relating the incident led to a discussion of personal arms, state laws, and permits. We also talked about types of handguns for everyday concealed carry and the overriding requirement that the gun not be one that can go off if dropped.

I told him of one hazard that is beyond comprehension for those to whom firearms are alien objects. That is that the weapon becomes as much a part of one's accouterments as wristwatch, pen, and wallet. For those of us who spend a lot of time around airports, the problem is obvious. Every now and then, someone punctuates the boredom of an airport security guard's life by forgetting to disarm himself or herself before walking through the metal detectors.

We talked about the heavy responsibility a citizen who chooses to keep a weapon close at hand must assume, the absolute necessity of keeping the gun where children can't get at it.

My friend asked what I thought of the idea of carrying a gun. I said that, the way the world is now, it may be foolish not to—if a carrier is willing to learn how, when, and when not to use it, and *if* that person is willing to bear responsibility for having at hand the means to take an innocent life as easily as a threatening one.

According to the only extensive study of the subject, American citizens use personal arms to prevent crimes nearly a million times a year. My friend and his wife may have prevented one merely with luck and a hint they might have been armed. Next time they won't rely on luck.

Letter to an anti-hunter

D ear Correspondent,

Yours is the only one of many letters that I've received over the years objecting to my thoughts on hunting that bore a signature. The only unsigned letters I've received are from people objecting to my enjoyment of hunting and to my views on animal "rights". I offer that for what it's worth.

I did not write in my June 4 column that all observers of nature are fanatics. I said that animal rights fanatics *come from* that group; people who blow up animal testing laboratories and "liberate" animals from zoos are not the same people who enjoy hunting and fishing.

Your rural background gives you a broader field of reference than does mine. While I am painfully aware of the large number of hunters to whom the kill is the only reward of the hunt, they are not the people I hunt with.

I have more contact with hunting and hunters through literature than I do from experience. The kinds of jerks and slobs you describe are not the ones who write and publish their outdoor experiences and the thoughts that accompany those experiences.

I do not believe, as you do, that all life has an equal "right" to exist. If life were sacred, nature would not be so wasteful of it. Predators would not exist. Disease would not exist. Overpopulation leading to destruction of habitat and subsequent starvation would not exist.

Fish would spawn only enough eggs to reproduce their species, not thousands of times that number only to see ninety-nine percent of them not reach maturity because of predation. Wolves

81

would not exist to kill calves of caribou and elk. Coyotes woul
not exist to kill mice and rabbits, and mice and rabbits would nc
reproduce by millions to ensure that coyotes can eat most of ther
yet leave enough to make more rabbits and mice to feed mor
coyotes.

As for zoos, what is wrong with animals living in man-mad
recreations of their natural environments in which they hav
modern health care to take care of their ills, kill (there's that wor
again) their parasites, and protect them from predators tha
would eventually kill them in their natural world?

I don't consider those who believe as you do to be fanatics jus
because of those beliefs. Fanatics tear down fences at min:
farms, pour paint on people who wear fur coats, bomb medica
research laboratories that use animals, and prefer to see animal
die of starvation rather than be shot by hunters. They woul
rather that surplus animals be killed by government gunmei
than by sport hunters solely because hunters might enjo
themselves doing it.

So I don't consider you a fanatic from anything in your letter
but I'm curious: Do you swat the mosquito that bites you or th
fly that lights on your table? Do you try to kill fleas and mite
that torment your pets, if, indeed, you allow yourself pets?

Are your beliefs consistent? Do you hold hunters in equa
contempt with the bats that kill and eat mosquitoes, the gull
that kill and eat locusts, the cats that kill and eat mice, th
robins that kill and eat worms, the trout that kill and ea
mayflies, the whales that kill and eat krill, and all fish in the se:
that kill and eat other fish?

Do you refuse to take antibiotics to kill the bacteria that mak
you ill, refuse to kill germs by washing your hands and clothe:
with soap or detergent or by brushing your teeth? Do you refrair
from cleaning a child's scraped knee before bandaging it becaus
it might deny infecting microbes the right to fester and propagat
at the child's expense?

Yes, I'm bordering on the absurd here, but if a line of thought
when carried to its logical extreme, becomes absurd, perhaps i
indicates a flaw in the line of thought.

The natural world seems based on a shifting balance betweer
predator and prey. The concept of life as sacred is a humar
invention.

Make 'em mad, they'll get even

The telephone woke me at three in the morning. It rang only once. I sat up in bed, heart pounding in reaction to the jangling noise, and tried to decide if it had been the phone or the alarm clock. Maybe it was nothing.

"Who is it?" Barb asked.

"Did the phone ring?" I asked.

"I thought you answered it," she said.

"I thought maybe I dreamed it," I said.

I fumbled around and found the phone. "Hello?" Dial tone. I rolled over and went back to sleep.

"I'll bet it was the lady at the magazine getting even," my stepmother said at breakfast. She, too, had been awakened.

The lady at the magazine. That would never have occurred to me. I'd decided the single ring was the result of some electronic gremlin on the line, or perhaps a call from someone who realized at the last moment that the number had been misdialed. But at three o'clock in the morning?

Fumble-fingered drunks ring up wrong numbers an hour earlier when the bars close and they're inclined to stay on the line and argue. I began to consider that the call may indeed have come from the lady at the magazine.

I can tolerate telephone solicitation, even though I don't like it. I try to be polite, even when the calls come, as they always seem to, during naps and meals.

The conversations usually run like this:

"Good evening, Mr Rush, howya doin' this evening?"

That's the tip-off. The only people who ever say "howya doin'" on the telephone in the first sentence are selling something.

"What are you selling?" I ask.

They hate to admit they're selling anything. They prefer to say they're "offering" something. Most often lately it's pre-approved Visa cards. That's an easy one to take care of. I tell the caller I have a no-fee card at under eleven percent and ask if they can beat it. They can't, of course, and that usually takes care of that.

One enterprising credit card "offerer" said he could beat my rate. No fee and nine-point-something.

"What's the catch?"

"No catch."

"Okay, how long does that rate last?"

"Uh, well, six months."

"And then what is it?"

"Uh, well, fourteen-point-nine percent."

I politely say, "No thank you," and hang up.

We were having a late dinner on the last day of my parents' Christmas visit when the lady at the magazine called.

I can't ignore a ringing telephone during holiday seasons when far-flung friends and family members are likely to call, so when the lady at the magazine called, I got up from the table and answered it:

"Hello."

"Is this Eric Rush?"

"Yes it is," I said, and tried to match the voice to someone I know.

Nope. She was calling on behalf of a consumers' magazine we subscribe to and support with additional donations now and then. I didn't give her time to explain what the pitch was this time. "You've caught me in the middle of dinner," I said, not unkindly.

"Oh, I'm sorry. May I call back at a more convenient time?"

"Sure," I said.

"When would be a good time?"

My mouth said, "How about nineteen-ninety-seven or -eight?"

There was half a second of silence before she spoke again, exasperated this time, no longer cheerful. "What an idio—" she said, the last word chopped off by a hard click and silence. Maybe I was one smart alec too many for her that day.

I'll never know if she called in the night to get even. I wouldn't blame her if she had.

I'd resolved to make no New Year's resolutions, but I've broken that one already.

I resolve in the new year always to be polite to telephone solicitors, to avoid making their jobs more miserable than they already are. I further resolve to give thanks that I don't have to make a living in such a thankless occupation.

Playing God, or not?

The death of Sue Rodriguez in Victoria this week brought the issue of doctor-assisted suicide geographically closer to home. It may be, however, that Sue Rodriguez died a more natural death than if she'd been kept alive until even the maximum effort of medical science could no longer keep her wasted body warm.

To many, suicide in any circumstance is appalling. That some medical professionals help their patients leave this life is worse. A common cry in opposition even to letting the terminally ill die, much less helping them, is that human beings have no right to "play God".

We have been playing God since we first learned to heal sickness, prevent infection, and to splint broken bones. It is not playing God to pull the plug on the respirator of a comatose patient; it is playing God to plug it in.

The life cycle, in simple form, is to be born, to procreate, and to die. Some insects manage all that in so short a time they don't even have to eat. Generally, the more advanced the life form, the longer it takes to do those things, but once that destiny is fulfilled, life, biologically, becomes waiting to die.

Modern human beings aside, the last arc of the life cycle is fairly short. When the deer can no longer withstand the privations of winter, it dies. When the cougar can no longer catch its prey, it dies. Animals die when they can no longer, on their own, perform the functions that sustain their lives.

Except for us.

Some primitive (by our standards) peoples allow their elders to die when they become too frail to keep up with tribal migrations or when there is not enough food for everyone, but most of us seem to accept with little or no thought that the purpose of human life is to make it last as long as possible regardless of quality, regardless of cost, and regardless of the burden it may place on others.

Ernest Hemingway was one of my youthful heroes. When he killed himself thirty-three years ago, when he was only ten years older than I am now, I felt more than sad at the death of someone I greatly admired; I felt betrayed. I felt, at first, that he had chickened out of life, that he wasn't able to fill his own shoes. But it wasn't long before I came to believe that Hemingway had died a natural death.

He had completed his life's cycle. He was born, he grew up, he had children, and he'd contributed more to literature than most writers ever had or ever will. Though still not old by modern standards, he was old by natural law and by his own expectations of himself.

His mind would no longer arrange the words the way it once had, so his primary human reason for living had ended. He had already done the things that most of us put off for our retirement years. He'd lived wherever he'd wanted to live, written everything he was able to write, hunted everything there was to hunt, fished for everything there was to catch, and when he had done all those things and could do no more, he allowed himself to die.

Hemingway, being a modern man and living in a modern world, did not walk out into a cold night to let his life heat drain from him back to the earth. He did not succumb to combat with a younger, stronger member of his species as an old lion might have done, but his death was more natural than it would have been had he lived until today, passing time in a nursing home, far from the natural world he was a part of, taking pills on schedule and having his diapers changed.

Sue Rodriguez was doomed to waste away and die of Lou Gehrig's Disease, her pain eased by narcotics, unable to speak, unable to move, ultimately unable to live. She refused to allow her government to play God with her. She ended her life while she still had a life to end. Ended it bravely. Ended it with dignity. Ended it in the company of courageous friends.

Whether to live as long as possible or to die as well as possible should be an individual choice. It is not for us, the young and healthy, to decide for the sick and infirm.

Market hunting, market fishing

The time has come for a total and permanent ban on commercial fishing for salmon and other game fish whose numbers are declining fast. Sport fishing must also be severely restricted or even halted until fish populations recover.

The plight of game fish today is similar to that of game animals at the end of the last century. Market hunting had driven bison, beaver, elk, and some birds to the brink of extinction just as market fishing has endangered salmon and steelhead. Abolition of commercial hunting and regulation of sport hunting was instrumental in bring back game populations, in many cases to levels far above what they were before the European invasion of North America.

While there are parallels between the situations of game animals a century ago and game fish now, there are also differences.

While we slaughtered game animals without thought to the future, we also slaughtered their predators. While we destroyed animal habitat with our domestication of the land, we also created diversity of habitat by breaking up forests and planting grain. It was both that increased diversity of habitat and the reduction of predators that allowed deer and elk, among others, to rebound to the degree they have.

Deer, once scarce, are now pests in parts of the country. Now there is growing pressure to bring back the traditional predator, the wolf, in part to counterbalance the exploding deer populations.

The pattern of game animal decline and recovery differed from that of fish in some respects.

Just as animal populations declined because of commercial hunting and habitat destruction, so have fish.

Light & Dark

The cod fishery in the North Atlantic was sustained for three hundred and fifty years and wiped out in ten by increasingly efficient technology and failure of nations to agree on adequate regulation.

It is not just commercial fishing that is to blame for the plight of salmon, of course. While we exterminated wolves and cougars to the best of our ability as we were slaughtering their prey, we began over-protecting the marine mammals that prey on fish. Understanding of the effect of dams on salmon propagation came after the dams were built. The effects of logging on spawning streams are only now starting to be understood.

It is too late to do anything about large dams. It will take time to mitigate the effects of harmful logging practices. Shooting a few sea lions will help in isolated instances, but it may be impossible to change the laws and re-establish regulated commercial sealing. But fishing can be halted now.

It's difficult to face major changes in the way we live. We see that first hand in the despair and bewilderment of our friends and neighbors in the timber industry who have, through no fault of their own, had their way of life yanked from under them by changes in the way we value trees. We can imagine that people a hundred years ago who earned their livings and supported their families by selling fur and hides and meat must have felt the same when the government told them they could no longer live as they and their parents had. It will be at least as hard on the hardy, independent souls who live by the ancient traditions of fishing the seas. And it will be hard on the tribes who have always netted the rivers and who, had Europeans not come here, could have continued to net them forever.

It will be hard on all of us when we run out of oil and have to give up our cars. It will be harder still if the human population of the earth continues to explode and deprives all of us of health, food, peace, and prosperity. All major changes in the ways we live are hard.

It will be hard for commercial salmon fishermen to fish no more. It will be hard for the rest of us to hang up our rods for a year or two or ten. But if we want the fish to recover so that we can again catch them on hook and line on Summer mornings and know that our children and their children can do the same, we must stop the market hunting of fish now and, perhaps, forever.

Bargain hat? It's a Stihl

It's my favorite hat. I've worn it every for years. It's a warm, snug, knit hat, bright orange and white with a white pompon on top. In black block letters on the white band it says Stihl. My wife hates it.

I didn't know she hates it until last weekend when we went to the outdoor sports show in the Kingdome. A white-haired man running the chainsaw winch booth noticed my hat. "You don't see those anymore," he said. "They're rare."

Rare? My promotional hat I got free when I bought my first Stihl chainsaw a dozen years ago? Or was it when I bought a Honda outboard from the same dealer a few years later? I wasn't sure.

It's always been just a hat, one of several in my closet—watch caps, one-size-fits-all promotional caps, and a battered Stetson. Sometimes I've temporarily lost it for a few days or weeks, but it always turns up somewhere eventually, on the sailboat maybe, or in my truck. I'm always happy to find it, but it's not something I spent time worrying about. Not until someone said it was rare. That's when my wife said she hates it.

We wandered around the show for a couple of hours, looking at the latest in fishing gear, entering drawings for trips to fishing and hunting lodges all over North America, and trying to resist the temptation to spend money. But all that time, I was thinking about my hat. Sometimes rare means valuable. I couldn't leave until I'd found out more.

The old man was still at the winch display. I told him I'd been worrying about what he'd said about my hat, that after all the years I'd worn it without thinking about it, now I was afraid of losing it. It's a good hat, but if it's too valuable to wear, I wanted to know it.

Light & Dark

He didn't have much to add to what he'd already said, just that people who have those Stihl chainsaw hats keep them, the ones that haven't disappeared over the years. He didn't offer to buy mine and I didn't offer to sell it.

While walking out to our car, I was conscious of the bright orange hat perched on my head. I wondered if there were collectors out there with an eye peeled for just such a hat, the same kind of people that always check their pocket change for Indian head pennies and liberty dimes. I wondered if, unknown to me, there was a hat collector's society, unnoticed and perhaps unscrupulous, that was the cause of the occasional disappearance of those hats we all lose from time to time and assume we've misplaced or given to Goodwill.

I tried to read on the ferry as I drank my coffee, but I couldn't concentrate on my book. I felt conspicuous in my orange hat. I felt tighter than usual, heavier. I was constantly aware that it was on my head. I took it off and set on the table and resisted the impulse to look around to see if any of the other passengers seemed to be taking an unusual interest in it.

I went to sleep that night thinking about it. When I awoke in the morning, I forced myself not to check in the closet to be sure it was still there. Not until after breakfast, anyway.

It was one of two hats I got over the years from Port Angeles Chain Saw. The other, a bedraggled red baseball cap, I got either when I bought the saw or the outboard. It looked older than the Stihl hat, but I couldn't remember, so I drove to Port Angeles with both of them to find out.

It's Port Angeles Power Equipment now, but the owners are the same. I told Mike the story of the hat he'd given me years before and asked if he knew which hat I got when and if the knit Stihl hats were still available. He didn't, but Susie did. The hat was a Christmas promotion at least ten years ago, a one-time deal, so it is the older of the two. I've had it more than twelve years, longer than any other hat I own.

I'll keep wearing it, of course. Worrying about losing it will be easier than trying to explain keeping it in a safety deposit box in a bank.

I asked my wife why she hates my hat. She said if I don't know, I'll never understand. She's probably right. I don't even understand what she said.

Why the innocent are executed

The best argument against capital punishment is not that it makes society a murderer or that it is inhumane. The best argument is that sometimes innocent people are executed. Widely publicized cases of wrongful convictions being reversed strengthen that argument. But there are three easily identifiable factors that send innocent people to prison and to death that can and must be rectified for justice to prevail in capital and non-capital cases.

The first and most pervasive is the unwarranted reliance on eyewitness identification. The second is credence given to testimony of those who stand to gain by their testimony. The third—less common, I hope—is absolutely intolerable. That is the fabrication, manipulation, and suppression of evidence by those responsible for seeing justice done.

Memories of things seen and heard are not recordings. They are only impressions and are easily influenced by external suggestion. Yet such is our faith in "I know what I saw" that juries often accept eyewitness testimony over physical evidence that contradicts it.

That prosecutors and juries lend any credence whatsoever to statements by criminals and suspects about "knowledge" they claim to have about an accused person is beyond comprehension. A common form is testimony from criminals facing long prison terms in exchange for lenient treatment. These paragons of virtue swear on Bibles and their mothers' graves that the accused

91

confessed to them in jail. Juries believe them, and innoce people go to prison.

Most abhorrent, most inexcusable, and absolutely unacceptab is manipulation of evidence by representatives of the crimir justice system.

It isn't impossible to understand why a cop might plant dru on a suspect he "knows" is bad. Neither is it impossible understand why a prosecutor might neglect to mention facts th point toward a defendant's innocence.

Imagine the frustration of a police officer when, over and ov again, he sees bad guys back on the street soon after valid arres and convictions. Imagine the temptation of a prosecutor, certa in his own mind that an accused is guilty in spite of inconclusi or contradictory evidence, to strengthen his case by suppressi facts that might give a jury reasonable doubt.

Though we can perhaps understand, we must not accept the abuses of basic rights. We can expect criminals to swear false but the good guys must not. The search for truth must alwa supersede desire for conviction.

So what should be done?

When an accused is convicted because hard facts and complete web of circumstantial evidence leave no reasonal alternative, make him serve his sentence. All of it. Don't let hi go back on the street to insult, by his presence, the integrity a devotion of the police officers who arrested him. Don't tempt t prosecution to cheat a little to put him away for good.

Juries must be made aware of the fallibility of eyewitne testimony. Prosecutors must not rely upon it for convictio when it is at odds with better evidence.

Make perjured testimony punishable by triple the maximu sentence the accused is subject to. And if the accused fac possibility of execution, let the perjurer who tried to send him his death be executed.

The same should hold for those who suppress, manufacture manipulate evidence. If overzealous officials are found to ha caused an innocent person to be convicted by their intention improper actions or omissions, free the innocent and let tl prosecutors, police officers, or any other justice system officia serve triple the falsely convicted's sentence. If that mea sending them to the gallows, so be it.

wo dead deer

Both deer died because trucks hit them on highways, but they could not have died more differently. One was a two-point ck, antlers still in velvet. He was old enough to have had perience crossing highways, but his luck ran out one evening is Summer. The other was a newborn fawn that died on a untry road in the Midwest last Spring.

he old pickup that hit the buck probably did so accidentally, hough the driver didn't stop. The driver may not have thought e deer was badly hurt when a glancing blow to its hindquarters ocked it down, but he should have stopped to find out.

he buck dragged itself off the highway with forelegs only, his id legs dragging at odd angles. My wife and I pulled off into a ivel parking area where the deer was struggling to get up and n. I got out and walked near, slowly, talking low and soft. The er settled down and lay still, his head up and watching me.

t first I saw no outward sign of injury, other than the responsive hind legs. I hoped he was only stunned, but then I w large splashes of blood on the ground and a gaping wound on e hindquarter.

couldn't remember whether it is legal to kill a mortally injured d suffering game animal in this state, but I didn't much care. I : my pistol from the car, told the deer I was sorry, and shot it ough the brain.

Light & Dark

Killing things is not pleasant to me, even when it's necessary. knelt there beside deer for a few moments as the light faded from its eyes, then drove home and called the State Patrol.

I called to report the incident mostly because I wanted the state to have the opportunity to collect the fresh carcass if it was still policy to use fresh roadkill in prison mess halls. But I also wanted to know if what I'd done was legal. The dispatcher said the Department of Wildlife has no objection to killing injured animals as an act of mercy. It was some small comfort to know that what I believed to be the morally right thing to do was also legally right.

When I told this story to a man I was flying with last week, he told me the story of the fawn.

Mike was driving along a two-lane country road near his Indiana farm one day last Spring with his brother who was visiting from California. A doe stepped into the road some distance ahead and crossed. Mike slowed down in case there were more deer hidden in the grass and trees. He stopped his car when a fawn, following its mother on awkward, untried legs, staggered into the road and fell in front of the car.

Mike was just about to get out to help the fawn cross the road when it got up and continued on its own into the other lane.

The pickup coming around the curve had plenty of time to stop If the driver had wanted to. He could even have moved onto the shoulder and gone on by.

The fawn fell again, still on the pavement, in plain view of the oncoming driver who carefully lined up his truck and ran over the struggling fawn with front and rear left wheels and killed it.

Mike is a tough man, but he was horrified as well as enraged. "If I'd had a gun, I'd have shot him," he said to me, and I do not believe he exaggerated. His brother could not believe what he'd seen, that a human being had deliberately smashed the life out of a newborn deer for nothing but the sheer hell of it.

Neither man got the license number or even a good description, but they called the police anyway. Nothing the police could do they said, even if they could have found the driver. No law in that state that makes running over animals a crime.

We say it takes all kinds of people to make a world. Maybe that's why the world is the kind of place it is. Maybe it would be a better world of some kinds of people were never born.

Of beaks and teeth

If I'd had a vote on the course of human evolution a few million years ago, I think I'd have chosen a beak over teeth. That thought formed in response to a couple hours of dental maintenance this week that, while necessary if I want my teeth to last as long as I do, was not pleasant. Maybe I'll feel better when I can go back to solid food.

Imagine the advantages of simple beaks over the complex mechanism of teeth and gums. We wouldn't need toothpicks and floss. Unruly people would be less inclined to smack us in the mouth.

Eating would be simpler without the need for myriad utensils. All we'd need is a big bowl at each place and a stick to hold down one end of things like steaks while we ripped off a hunk with a deft twist of the head. An indicator of manners and breeding, instead of how we hold our forks, might be the style with which we ripped our meat. Perhaps a graceful, hardly noticeable twitch would indicate upper-class origins while a violent yank with accompanying splatters of gravy would give away those of lesser breeding.

Washing down the meal with water or wine would be trickier. Perhaps the style would be to tilt one's head back and open wide and pour liquid down the gullet from a traditional glass. Or perhaps we'd find it simpler to use plastic squeeze bottles to squirt the Chardonnay to the back of the beak.

The advantages to having beaks instead of teeth would lie in reduced maintenance. No cavities to drill and fill, no plaque to scrape, no gums to bleed. The disadvantages would probably outweigh them.

Without lips and teeth, speech patterns would be different. We'd either sound like talking parrots or sing and whistle to communicate. George Bush would not have said "Read my lips" and might still be president.

Having beaks would definitely take the fun out of kissing. The expression, "a peck on the cheek" would have a more literal meaning. The history of popular music would not read as it does. No ruby lips. No "Kisses Sweeter Than Wine". A more likely romantic song title might be, "Beakause You're Mine".

The lipstick industry would not have come into being. Beakstick? Maybe so, but to what purpose? Of course, the same could be asked of lipstick.

Men would not wear mustaches simply because there would be no place to grow them.

Plastic surgery to improve the appearance of one's face would be simpler and cheaper. No longer would surgeons have to remove nasal cartilage, file down bone, and stitch skin back together with such exacting care that no scars would show. A beak job might be a do-it-yourself project. All you'd need would be a small saw, sandpaper, and a tube of glue.

We must have evolved teeth instead of beaks for a reason, even though beaks seem simpler. Teeth may increase the chances for individual survival. Break a tooth and you can still eat. Break your beak and you might have starved, back in the days before super glue.

If I were thirty years older, I might not bother with long-term tooth maintenance. Why undergo discomfort and expense to make my teeth last longer than I will? For that matter, now that you can get false teeth for a few bucks at your corner denturist in Washington, why not have all the troublesome, cavity-prone natural teeth removed now and replaced with good old reliable plastic?

Some people do that. I know a man in Kentucky who had all his teeth pulled in late adolescence. His dentures fit perfectly the first time and still do. Others aren't so lucky.

Since trading troublesome teeth for a beak is not an option, I'll continue to let the dental surgeon whittle and whack and slice and scrape for a couple more sessions, but not until after Thanksgiving. And after that, I think I'll go in for my annual teeth cleaning every six months instead of every few years.

Prohibition folly, then and now

The parallels between the nationwide prohibition of alcohol early in this century and the present prohibition of drugs are too great to ignore. Both prohibitions were and are extremely expensive. Both, in their widespread lack of unanimous public support, were unenforceable.

Frustrated police agencies at all government levels became riddled with corruption in both instances. Increased efforts to enforce the unenforceable led to decreased respect for civil rights of all citizens. Both prohibitions created massive criminal organizations. Both prohibitions were and are utter failures.

We finally came to our senses as a nation and abandoned the prohibition of alcohol after only a few years. It is time for us to abandon the prohibition of drugs. Prohibition as a cure for a social ill is worse than the disease.

The war on drugs has forced the dope business to make bulky, relatively mild forms of drugs into concentrates that are easier to conceal. Instead of cocaine powder—at one time the "coke" in Coca-Cola and an ingredient in many over-the-counter remedies—we have crack. Instead of opium—a relatively benign drug—we have the far more potent heroin. In addition to the mild marijuana leaf, we have the concentrate hashish.

HL Mencken summarized results of the national prohibition of alcohol in 1922 after just three years: Loss of tax revenue from the legal sale of alcohol was half a billion dollars a year. Annual cost to the government of maintaining an army of prohibitio agents was fifty million dollars. Illegal revenue generated k bootlegging and illegal manufacture of alcohol was in th neighborhood of one billion dollars a year. Supplies for hom brewing, distilling, and winemaking became a huge busines: The attempted prohibition of alcohol became a national jok Every known alcoholic beverage was available almost everywher but at up to five times the pre-prohibition prices and untaxed.

Evading prohibition quickly evolved a national sport, Mencke wrote. Public perception idolized the bootlegger and saw goverr ment prohibition agents as the villains.

Probably nothing degrades the spirit of police officers more tha their perception that the public does not support their efforts an doesn't see them as the good guys. If we don't see them as th good guys, they have less incentive to remain good guy: especially when bad guys make so much more money.

If we don't care, why should the police? If society supports th huge illegal drug industry with dollars, even while we preac against it, why should police officers risk their lives fighting it?

Our sense of proportion has become distorted. We ofte sentence those convicted of drug offenses to longer terms than w do murderers, robbers, and rapists. We take out frustration a our inability to convict and imprison the leaders of the dru cartels by coming down with both feet on an individual who grow a couple of marijuana plants in his house because smoking eases the symptoms of disease. We are trying to put out gras fires while our civilization burns out of control.

There are those who say we must continue the war on drug because to end it would be to admit defeat. We said the sam thing about the war in Vietnam as our soldiers continued to die.

There are those who say that to stop fighting against drugs i the same as condoning their use, that legalizing their use wi increase the numbers of people who use them. But many peopl became drinkers during prohibition simply to defy prohibition, fo the thrill of daring to do something illegal. And we did nc become a nation of alcoholics when Prohibition was repealed.

Abuse of alcohol is not good for individuals or for society, bu prohibition did not eliminate alcohol use or abuse.

Neither is abuse of drugs good for individuals and for societ; but prohibition, as with alcohol, only makes the problems worse.

Our new cultural taboo

Firearms are replacing sex as our great cultural taboo. Nothing else explains the profusion of irrational attitudes and meaningless legislation blooming like algae in these times.

The youth movement of the 1960s brought crashing down the crumbling wall of sexual taboo that had stood from the time of the Puritans. Nature, including human nature, abhors a vacuum. We are filling that cultural vacuum with a transcendent fear of firearms.

Everyone has always known about sex, but until recently, no one wanted to admit that it existed or, if it did, that they thought about it. Not admit it officially, that is. Not publicly. To enforce, officially, our denial of sex and our public disgust with the very idea of it, we passed unenforceable laws regulating private sexual behavior. We insisted at various times that different parts of the human body be covered, parts that, if seen, would excite sexual lust and remind us that the urge did, indeed, exist.

Preachers preached against sexual lust. Social and religious moralists set strict guidelines for the practice of sex. Children had to be protected from knowledge of and exposure to it.

Suppression of interest and knowledge leads to irrational fear and obsession. So it has been with sex. So it is becoming with firearms.

Sex existed in spite of denial. Imaginative bedroom activity continued in spite of laws against it. But the laws stood because they reflected the cultural taboo. The facts that they were ineffective and caused even greater interest in the outlawed activity were denied or ignored.

Light & Dark

Laws and attitudes in opposition to sexual behavior that cause harm are good for society and for individuals. So are laws and attitudes in opposition to misbehavior with firearms.

At the same time society is coming to the realization that educating children about sex lessens their obsession with it and reduces the risk that they will harm themselves and each other with it, there is only a small minority that urges similar education about that other fact of American life—guns. We teach about sex to counteract the misinformation and distorted perceptions that movies and television expose us to, but we do nothing to correct and counteract distortions of the use of firearms that entertainment media depends on almost for its very existence.

At the same time Congress wants to hand out condoms like candy, it also wants to stop its long-standing program of providing ammunition to school gun clubs and other organizations that teach safe recreational shooting.

As the fall of sexual taboos began in New York and California and spread inland, so too is the new taboo arising in those states and spreading inland. Perhaps the cultural influence of the recent influx of Californians into Washington is partly responsible for the latest state legislation helping establish firearms as taboo.

One aspect of enforcing taboos is to hide from view reminders that the taboo activity exists. In colonial times, even an exposed ankle was scandalous. Now that the sex taboo has fallen, exposure of nearly every bit of skin is ho-hum. So what do we do? We hide guns.

New state law says, "no person may carry a firearm unless it is...enclosed in an opaque case...or...wrapper." The guns are still there, but the state doesn't want people to see them.

There are so many exceptions written into that law that it applies to almost no one and in almost no situations, but the law is on the books, and that is the main thing. The new taboo has legal standing.

The legislators must have felt properly embarrassed by their efforts, because they allow "any city, town, or county" to exempt itself from this law.

Meanwhile, many of us risk violation of state law every time we cross a city or county line in our trucks with rifles or shotguns in the gun rack. Unless, of course, they're properly covered. Like Hester Prynne's ankles.

Reunions: a second chance

think I may have figured out why some of us love high school
reunions and others do not. I haven't missed one yet. I'll go to
nem as long as I'm alive and as long as there is one other of us
live and able to attend.

Last week was the thirty-five-year reunion for my Boulder,
olorado, class of 1960. I almost missed it.

I think the reason we held it on Friday and Saturday instead of
n both weekend days may have been out of consideration for the
ıct that it takes old folks longer to recover from excessive
elebration. Whatever the reason, work kept me from Friday's
estivities and those of the following morning. I tried to make up
or it Saturday night.

Some people don't much care for reunions. Perhaps they have
ved their lives more satisfactorily from day to day and from year
ว year than I have. Perhaps their high school days were just as
njoyable as their lives since then, but I am a happier person now
ıan I was in my youth. My nostalgia for those past years is not
ว much that I want to relive my past; I long to go back and do it
ght.

At high school reunions, we feel acceptance that many of us did
ot feel as teenagers. I was one of those self-conscious, socially
nskilled misfits who was not a part of the crowd. At least that's
ie way it seemed at the time. My yearbook lists only one activity
nder my name, and I doubt I attended more than one meeting of
ven that one club.

Rather than try to overcome shyness and make an effort learn
ow to be social, I took the easy way out and hung around with

others of similar disposition, those with little aptitude for athletics, those who had not learned and perhaps never would learn how to be part of a team of any sort.

And the kicker is—laughable now in its self-deception—the problem wasn't ours, we believed. It was theirs. Those socially adept members of clubs and teams and honor rolls and student councils who stood straight and walked proudly were stuck up. They ran around in their little cliques and ignored those of us not their social equals. That's what we believed, those of us on the sidelines in our own scruffy little groups who made no effort to join with those whom we secretly felt superior to and even more secretly envied.

It was probably the twenty-year reunion before I began to realize that I had had no monopoly on insecurity, that perhaps others had been as afraid of me as I had been of them, that girls I was afraid even to talk to might have been pleased had I asked for a date. It is only now, in recent years, that it has begun to sink in that kids like me appeared as standoffish and as stuck up to others as they did to us.

So when I walk into the banquet room on for the dinner and dance on the last evening of the reunion, and people I hardly knew and have not seen in years greet me with no less delight and enthusiasm than do old friends who are there, it's an opportunity for me to relive, a little bit, that time long past when I did not get as much out of life as I should have because I did not put as much into it as I should have.

And so I eat and drink and dance and talk and laugh. I feel like Cinderella, knowing midnight will come and wanting the clock to stop, just for a little while, And, because time is limited, I try to cram as much as possible into those few hours.

Because I want to talk to everybody, I don't listen enough to anybody. And because I'm exhausted from having flown all night and having been up most of the day, I have another drink or two to keep me going, forgetting that fatigue and Colorado's altitude make a little alcohol go a long way. Yes, it is good planning to have the reunion end on Saturday, not Sunday.

I think perhaps some who love reunions do so because they want to recall a happy time of their lives, but others of us love them because they allow us to enjoy a taste of something we missed the first time around.

3lind date with an old friend

' guess you could call him a pen pal, though I've never thought . of him that way. It seems too casual a label to apply to this ıan a generation older than I, a man I'd never met or spoken to ho who has been a friend for nearly thirty years.

My introduction to him came a couple of marriages ago. He'd ıown known my bride's family well since his college days when he :nted rooms in their home and became, in heart and spirit, one ʰ the family.

I still have my first written word from him, addressed not to me ut but to my fiancée, a brief post card from early 1968 wishing us ell well in one paragraph and mentioning "an artery that's not ınctioning as it should" in another.

He is a more prolific letter writer even than I. His correspon-ınce ʰence followed us as we moved from Colorado to Oregon and New ʰexico and back to Colorado and on to Washington. Letters to ım him from both of us kept him informed of our adventures and ʰisadventures through the years of our marriage. I probably ave have all of his letters in dusty cardboard boxes, unless some were st in a house fire years ago.

Ｔhis friend I'd never met knows me well. Exchanging letters can ʰ more intimate, more deeply personal, than chats over coffee or ʰross a backyard fence. He has followed my growth from barely ıt of my teens through my evolution into middle age. His ıinking and insights have, I'm sure, influenced my own.

So, too, have I been privy to his life. Through the years, I've ʰeaned from his letters scraps and pieces of who he is. Over ʰme, what began as a bare sketch of the man in my mind has filled out into something more like a full portrait of an artist, sculptor, and writer, son of a prominent painter, grandson of a preeminent philosopher and educator.

His heritage is rich, but that wealth in mind and spirit is cruelly balanced by genetic disposition toward weakness in the physical heart. Already my friend has reached the age at which his grandfather and his grandfather's brother died. Already he has lived years longer than his father. Already he has had surgery to prolong his life. Already he has suffered a stroke, and that on an anniversary of his father's death.

Through these years, no convenient opportunity to visit him has presented itself to me, no opportunity for us to meet, to see each other beyond exchanged photos over a quarter of a century, beyond impressions constructed from photos and letters. He lives at the other end of the country and is forbidden by doctors to fly.

There is some danger in finally meeting someone whom one feels he knows already. There is some fear that reality might not equal expectation. Perhaps it was this fear that caused me to avoid for so many years making an effort to visit him.

A change in my airline's routing last week put me in Boston for a long layover. I didn't know I'd be going there until only hours before I arrived.

I'd had his phone number for several years but had never used it. When I did, it was incorrect. I called information, but his number is not published.

I could have simply walked up to his door and knocked, but that seemed somehow unmannerly, too informal for the occasion. Instead I called my former brother-in-law in Portland and left a message. A few hours later, he called with the correct number.

It was too late to call that night, so I phoned the next day and heard his voice for the first time. We met for dinner just hours before I had to leave.

Each of us was different from what we'd expected, but only slightly. I'm taller than he'd envisioned, and his medical burden is not apparent. He is spry, energetic, and as lively physically as he is in thought and spirit.

Three hours spent over dinner in a fine Boston restaurant went by as fast as a hamburger at a fast-food joint. We talked as if we were old friends who hadn't seen each other in a long, long time.

Which is exactly what we are.

Eating too slowly? Who, me?

It may not have been the first time I'd been thrown out of a joint, but it was the only time I've ever been asked to leave a restaurant because I was eating too slowly. As Dave Barry says, I'm not making this up.

I usually eat too fast. I'm making an effort to slow down some in many areas of my life, and eating is one of them. I remind myself that it is not usually necessary to eat as though I were making a pit stop in the rat race of life.

Regardless of what kind of place I'm eating in, I pay attention to the crowd. If tables are full and people are waiting to sit down, I don't linger over after-dinner coffee. Neither do I eat faster than I want to just to vacate my table sooner. Sometimes, when I am alone and the restaurant is crowded and people are waiting to sit down, I tell the headwaiter that I would welcome another single at my table.

Some restaurants, by their decor and menu, almost demand a leisurely pace. In those places, gobbling down a meal would be as out of place as a ringing cell phone at a church service. I found such a place near our layover hotel on Long Island. I wouldn't want to eat there every day. Prices are high and the food is rich but unusually good. Eating there is what some people might call a dining experience".

The restaurant was only half full when I went in for dinner. I ordered linguini with shrimp in a heavy cream sauce and began to read as I sipped coffee and ate my salad.

The food was not only rich, there was almost too much for one person. It was a meal to be savored, not gobbled.

As I read and ate, the restaurant filled and a line formed outside. My table was next to the window. I resisted the impulse

to hurry, although watching people shifting their weight from foo
to foot and glancing at their watches was a constant reminder no
to dawdle.

Maybe it was the fact that I was reading as I ate that made :
seem to the manager that I was taking forever and oblivious t
the waiting crowd. Maybe it was he who sent busboys over thre
times to try to take my unfinished meal from me.

I was full enough with only two or three bites remaining that
would have been better off leaving my plate unfinished, but tha
would have gone against the grain of my upbringing. There wer
nearly as many people outside as inside by then, and I was a
uncomfortable with the empty chair at my table as I was with m
overstuffed belly.

It's too bad the manager couldn't have waited two mor
minutes.

I don't remember his exact words, but he apologized fo
speaking to me, pointed out that he had people waiting, an
offered to buy my dinner if I'd leave.

It was New York, after all, but I was stunned.

I told him I was aware of the crowd, that I understood th
situation. I told him if I'd wanted fast food, I'd have gone t
McDonald's. "I will pay for my meal," I said, "and I will finish it."

He seemed uncomfortable. I certainly hope he was. I was no
going to let him salve his conscience by buying me off with th
price of dinner.

I pointed out that I was almost finished and would be in abou
three minutes. He went away. A moment later, my waitres
came by and asked if I'd like dessert. That presented a
opportunity I could not let pass.

I didn't want dessert and was too full to eat one anyway. But
replied to the waitress, not in a really loud voice, but not in a
whisper either, "Thank you, but no. Your boss thinks I'm eatin
too slowly and he's throwing me out. I'd like my check, please."

I don't know if the manager heard me, but people at nearby
tables did.

It was at least three more minutes before my check came and
that long again before the credit card slip came for me to sign.

The manager apologized again as I left and offered a free dinne
the next time I come in. I hope he's not keeping a table waiting.

Hunting and not hunting

The fat man stopped to gasp and wheeze and wipe sweat from his face. He wore bright new clothing and carried a muzzle-loading rifle. No binoculars hung from his neck and if he had any maps with him, any water, any anything, it wasn't apparent. The man gazed around as he stood in the gently sloping road sucking in air, looking for deer in the sage brush along the road, looking into the steep hills a person of his massive bulk and lack of conditioning could not climb. "You know," he said, "I took up deer hunting two years ago, and so far, I don't see what's fun about it."

Although he may have been the least prepared man we saw on the backroads west of Oroville earlier this month, he had plenty of company.

My partner and I parked our small trailer beside the road in an area we knew to be public land. We knew that because we have expensive forest service maps, color coded to show what is state, federal, reservation, and private land.

The only private land we considered hunting was a ranch posted with signs including a phone number to call for permission and information, a pleasant contrast to the stark, anonymous No Hunting and Keep Out signs most landowners post. We saved the number. Might want to call again next year before we go over there.

We spent time looking at our maps and studying the terrain in the area we thought looked good, public land with a corridor of public land for access. Grassy lower slopes with steep, rocky heights containing patches of pine forest. Reports of severe winterkill this year dampened our optimism, but our first day's foray into the hills confirmed the presence of deer.

Light & Dark

That first day of scouting further narrowed the type of terrain w should hunt. We'd seen little recent sign anywhere in the flat below the hills and none at all near the roads.

We explained all this to hunters who stopped their trucks to tal to us as we stood beside our trailer, drinking coffee, discussin strategy. Without telling them precisely where we were going t hunt, we told what we'd learned of where the deer were and how to get to them without infringing on private lands, posted or not.

Few of those we talked to had maps of any kind. Many looke as though they were just people out for a drive and who happene to have rifles along as an afterthought. Most of them cringe when we pointed across only a mile or two of sage and gras toward the steep hills where the deer were. Rather than spend few hours hiking to see for themselves, they all continued drivin slowly and peering into the flats and low hills beside the road as deer would be standing there waiting for someone to get out of truck to shoot them. Without binoculars, there could have bee deer there and the road hunters would never have seen them.

Although we saw almost no other hunters more than even half mile from a road, there were some. We saw a few and heard a occasional deep boom of black powder echoing through the hill and valley.

Our own hunt was successful, and would have been even if bot of us had missed our shots. It was successful in our mind because we located deer high on a distant mountain by sittin down on a nearby hill and spending time looking throug binoculars. We planned our stalk in detail and began ou approach.

It was a short stalk, not much more than an hour. The dee moved when I fired exactly the way we thought they would, an not only were there the three does and one buck we'd seen from below, there were six more bucks in the group that we hadn' seen. The ranges were better measured in feet than in yards. I doesn't get much better than that.

Hunters in cars and trucks continued to stop to talk as w packed the trailer and got ready to leave. Their eyes lit up whe we told them about all the deer we'd seen and dimmed agai when we pointed up into the hills. Then they continued slowl driving down the road that dozens of other hunters had jus driven and that dozens more would drive after them.

Education, if you will

She did not want to go to public high school. She absolutely did not. Don't be too quick to decide this thirteen-year-old is some sort of elitist snob who thinks she's too good to go to school with other kids in her neck of the woods. That isn't it at all.

Her family is neither rich nor poor. She does not live in a city. She lives in a log house full of books in rural New England with no television and attends public school in a small town nearby.

Our country is based, in large measure, on the idea that all of us should have equal opportunity in the pursuit of happiness. Public education in the United States is based on the idea that all citizens should have the opportunity to become educated. The key word in both cases is opportunity.

There is no guarantee of happiness in this country or in any other. There is no guarantee of success in one's chosen business profession or trade, and no guarantee that all will become equally educated.

There has been an increasing trend in my lifetime to misinterpret the ideal of equal opportunity as a government guarantee of equal result. We should all be equally wealthy, live in equally good neighborhoods, and be equally educated. What too few of us understand is that, if we all are to reach the finish line at the same time, we must all pace ourselves to the speed of the slowest runner. And if we all are to reach the end of our school years with the same level of education, we must all graduate at the level of the least educated.

In generations past, when one-room schools were a reality for many children, those of superior ability and those who were willing to work harder could not help but get ahead of their classmates.

Children born with a better brain than most and who acquired burning desire to climb out of the farm culture of the Texas Hill Country or the Nebraska Sand Hills might quickly finish school assignments and listen in on the studies of the older children in the single classroom. They might be moved up a grade level, or even two. They had no more opportunity to become educated than their classmates did; they simply made more of the opportunity.

Larger schools with only one grade level per classroom largely ended that. Education became more homogenized. Cream had less opportunity to rise to the top.

Public education too often limits opportunity to avoid the appearance of favoring brighter students. Too often it refuses to instill discipline to avoid attacks from those who refuse to accept discipline. Public education too often does disserve to the bright and motivated students by discriminating against them in favor of the mediocre. Often the only way to avoid wasting superior talent, industry, and intellect, is to opt out of public education and into private school.

In preparation for entering high school next year, the young lady's class took a guided tour of next year's school.

She definitely does not want to go there.

If her parents were rich, they might simply write a check for tuition to a good private school, but they are not rich, and I think they'd have the good sense not to do so even if money were no object. They told their daughter they could not afford private school, that if she wanted to go, she'd have to get a scholarship.

She did not whine or complain. She applied for scholarships, took tests, wrote essays. And she won a scholarship to one of the oldest and best prep schools in New England.

It's not a free ride, but it's close. Her parents will have to make some sacrifices to come up with the difference, but that's what parents are for.

She will get an education superior to most of the rest of the kids in her neck of the woods, but they have no call to complain. She earned it; they didn't.

A simple solution

This is a story you probably won't read in "Life in these United States" in *Reader's Digest*. On a layover in Seattle last week, one of my crewmembers rode the city bus from our hotel near the airport to the Pike Place Market to buy a fresh salmon to take home to New Hampshire.

Seattle buses have bike racks on the front, just as Clallam Transit buses do, but Seattle buses won't take bikes into the congested traffic of downtown or pick them up there. All bikes have to come off before the bus enters the no-bike zone.

This bus had one bicycle in the rack. The driver stopped at the first available stop and opened the door to let the bike owner out. But the young man who owned the bike either didn't understand the rule or didn't care. He refused to get off the bus and began arguing with the driver.

As the stalemated argument escalated and dragged on, some of the passengers began yelling at the young man to get off the bus so it could continue on its way, but he ignored them.

After what seemed like several minutes of shouting, one passenger reached the limit of his patience.

The problem may have been complicated by the fact that the young man with the bike was black. The driver was white, and the passengers were both. It was only black passengers who yelled at the young black man to get off; the whites remained silent.

Aside from a reasonable reluctance to become involved in a potentially violent situation, the whites were probably reluctant to involve themselves partly out of fear of young urban black men in general and partly out of fear of being considered racist for siding against any member of a racial minority for any reason. Certainly no white man in this modern age in a northern, cosmopolitan

111

metropolis would have dared end the impasse the way it wa
ended.

White people, other than out-and-out racists, often tend t
tolerate behavior among minorities that they would not amon
other whites. It may be condescension—a subtle form of racism-
that holds lower expectations for racial minorities in the sam
way we hold lower standards of behavior for children than fo
adults.

Or it may be a fear of appearing racist, of not thinking to ask o
of being unable to answer for oneself the question, "If that were
white man refusing to get off the bus, what would I think or sa
or do about it?"

A large black man solved the problem. He got out of his sea
walked to the front of the bus, and without a word, punched th
young black man in the face. Then he picked him up and thre
him out the door and onto the sidewalk. Next he stepped off th
bus, removed the bike from the rack, and threw it onto th
sidewalk.

Then he reboarded the bus and sat down again.

The applause was integrated and unanimous.

The driver closed the door and continued on his route.

If a white man had thrown a young white man off a Seattle bu
in identical circumstances, would the response of the passenger
black and white, been so favorable? Would whites and black
have reacted in the same way? If the troublemaker had bee
black, would the response have been the same had he bee
punched and thrown off by a white man? And what might th
reactions have been had a black man thrown a young white ma
off the bus?

And how would reactions have varied to each of these colo
combinations had the incident taken place in Detroit or Sa
Francisco or Minneapolis or Montgomery?

In a truly colorblind world, the response would be the same n
matter what the colors of those involved in any American city
although the cultures of some cities might be less tolerant of suc
sudden and direct unilateral problem solving. What might b
acceptable in Miami or Los Angeles might not be in Denver o
Dallas.

There must be a moral in here somewhere, but I haven't figure
out what it is.

A child passenger, not a pilot

One thing we need to get straight right now. Jessica Dubroff was not the pilot when the airplane she was in crashed any more than my eight-year-old daughter was when she and I flew our small Cessna across the country and back. Jessica may have been allowed to believe she was the pilot, but she was a passenger.

Had Katrina and I crashed enroute to Maine, you wouldn't have heard about it on network TV even once, much less for days on end. That's because we were on a vacation trip, not a media trip. We didn't think to tell NBC and the others we were going out to break some non-existent record.

Most airplane crashes occur, not because of one mistake or problem, but because several errors combine to make flight impossible. This one was no different.

The airplane Jessica was riding in did not crash just because it was overloaded. It did not crash just because the weather wasn't for anyone in any airplane to fly in. It did not crash just because airplanes don't perform as well at high altitude as at sea level. And it did not crash just because of any one of the other factors not yet known to us. But the overriding cause that includes many of the others is common. It's the one thing that probably kills more people in small airplanes than all other causes combined.

The first article I ever sold to a national aviation magazine dealt with this problem and was based on my own concerns as a flight instructor. The problem is simply that pilots take off when they should stay on the ground and continue when they should turn back. What's baffling is that if you could take them out of the wreckage, bring them back to life, and present to them th[...] circumstances existing at the time they made the decision th[...] killed them, they would not go. So why did they? Why d[...] Jessica's instructor, Joe Reid, take off?

It's one thing to sit here in our living rooms and look at all th[...] factors involved and say he should have waited until the stor[...] passed. If he were sitting here with us now, not in the front se[...] of that airplane with a schedule to meet and the eyes of the wor[...] watching him, I'm certain he would agree.

So what went wrong?

One thing that is not a cause is Jessica's age. She was to[...] young for a pilot's license, of course. But she was no more to[...] young to handle the controls of that airplane than my daught[...] was. There are two sets of controls. Control of the airplane as [...] practical and legal matter was in the hands of Joe Reid.

Aviation has a word for it: Get-there-itis. The disease afflict[...] amateurs mostly, but professionals are not immune. The urge t[...] get to a destination, to maintain a schedule, causes pilots t[...] ignore objective, rational decision-making. It killed Joe Reid an[...] his passenger.

Katrina's logbook shows nearly one hundred hours of fligh[...] time ending when she was eight years old, three times wh[...] Jessica Dubroff had. Does that mean she was three times [...] qualified as Jessica was? No. Katrina was in the front seat of o[...] airplane because two seats were all it had. We logged the tim[...] because we legally could and because a flight log makes a go[...] diary. And because she sometimes flew the airplane.

Katrina is grown now. I got a letter from her with her reactio[...] to Jessica Dubroff's death:

Why was it so important to break that record anywa[...] Shouldn't the love of flying be enough? ... It's one thing to have[...] child in love with flying and give her exposure to it. When I wa[...] her age, I thought it was perfectly normal to have a logbook ar[...] fly to Maine with my dad. But you never let me think, 'I can [...] that!'

To let a child that young think she can handle an aircraft in th[...] same way an adult could is just plain naive, stupid, and fatal.

May that little girl rest in peace.

Conversation, not confrontation

Anyone who spends a lot of time on the highway is more likely to be stopped for some infraction than someone who drives only a little.   Driving a couple thousand miles a month alertly, soberly, and doing everything right except pushing the speed just a bit will almost certainly result in getting stopped every few years, even though the driving itself is not unsafe.

I say this in attempt to portray myself as a safe driver who consistently cruises a bit faster than the dangerously boring fifty-five, not a reckless road warrior without regard for public safety.

It took a long time to get to a place I could get around some oblivious clown doing fifty down the highway east of Sequim while talking on his cell phone.   The law allows a driver in the act of passing on a two-lane highway to go over the speed limit, but it expects a reduction to legal speed as soon as safe after passing.

So it was, after passing on a downgrade and being behind schedule, that I was still well over the limit when I went around the next curve and saw the State Patrol car coming toward me.

A glance at my speedometer showed I was still at passing speed, so I naturally took my foot off the gas. I also naturally looked in the mirror.

The officer had turned around and was half a mile back, with lights on.   I didn't know if he wanted me to stop or was responding to an emergency call, so I slowed and eased over onto the paved shoulder. He did too.

I slowed even more and continued past the end of the guardrail and pulled off the road. Police work is dangerous enough without standing in the edge of the traffic lane to talk to errant drivers, so I always pull as far off as I can. I do that for the officer's safety.

After turning off the engine, I always sit still with my hands on the top of the steering wheel until the officer has come up, looked inside, and motioned to me to roll down the window. I do that for my safety.

Some psychologists claim it gives the person being stopped a psychological advantage to get out and walk to the police car. Meet the cop on his own turf. That might get you a psychological advantage, but it also might get you shot.

I assumed I was being stopped for speeding, but I wasn't certain enough to bet my life on it. If I were being stopped because a robber had just shot a store clerk and escaped in a small red pickup truck, imagine what might go through a police officer's mind if he saw me pull over and start rummaging around. I might be getting my registration out of the glove compartment or reaching into a coat pocket for my license, but I also might be reaching for a gun. So I sit still with my hands in plain view.

It occurred to me only later that never in my twenty-three years in Washington have I had to deal with unseen eyes behind mirrored sunglasses or an abusive manner from any police officer in any situation.

The patrol officer politely asked if I were aware of my speed. I said I was as soon as I saw him. I was surprised that he'd clocked me at precisely sixty-seven while going the opposite direction.

I offered no excuse, other than I was running late and had neglected to come back down to speed after passing the guy on the phone, and I promised to keep the speed down, and I did that.

No, I didn't get a ticket. And, yes, I got to the airport on time driving only three miles over the limit, except on Interstate Five where the legal sixty suits me fine.

Being treated as a fellow citizen, not as an adversary, made me feel that I'd be letting the officer down personally if I'd not kept my promise to slow down.

I don't know whether extreme courtesy is police policy in Washington, or whether I've been lucky over the years in dealing only with gentlemen, but police officers have always treated me with respect. I hope they're aware that the respect is mutual.

Coffee rules: part one

It wasn't a big enough misunderstanding to start a war, perhaps, but it was the sort of dispute that can lead to petty feuds and personal dislike. It was not an international dispute over oil or land or international treaty; it was two grown men getting hot under the collar over protocols of serving a cup of coffee.

One disadvantage of flying with an airplane loaded with boxes instead of people is that there are no flight attendants to serve coffee and snacks to the crew. We bring our own munchies and drinks—cookies, apples, peanuts, soft drinks, and coffee—and we share what we bring with the other two crewmembers.

The unwritten protocol at the airline I fly for is to set the box of cookies or bag of grapes on the radio console between the pilot seats where both pilots and the flight engineer can easily reach it. The donor often announces what is in the bag and invites the others to have some, but he doesn't really have to invite the others to partake of the goodies; it's understood that what's on the console is for consumption in common. However, when there is only one cookie left, no one wants to be the one to take it. It disappears only after polite discussion initiated by the person who brought it: *Somebody eat this last cookie...I've had my share, thanks...how about you?...no you go ahead...well, I guess somebody's gotta eat it.*

It's not exactly a Japanese tea ceremony, but the ritual serves a similar purpose: Politeness and established good manners lubricate human interaction and enable societies to run smoothly.

Light & Dark

I'm a coffee addict. I love the stuff and go to some inconvenience to be certain I have good coffee with me. Except for short flights, I carry a vacuum bottle and a ceramic mug.

Many of us like to drink coffee when it's available, but very few are willing to pack around a Thermos bottle of it, and I think I'm the only one of four hundred pilots at my airline to whom foam plastic cups are unacceptable.

I've been carrying coffee and sharing it with the crew for ten years. When I was a junior flight engineer, I also made sure there were plastic cups on the airplane for the captain and first officer, but I don't do that anymore. People who don't want coffee badly enough to be sure they have something to drink it out of can do without. What am I, their mother?

On long flights, I ration the coffee as if it were our only canteen on a trek across a desert. If all of us are coffee drinkers, we all do without until the halfway point. If one wants none, I open it sooner and pour the cups a little fuller. If I'm the only one who's drinking it, I drink as much as I want, when I want it, planning only to have one last cup remaining for near the end of the flight.

For these ten years, most of the pilots have waited patiently until I offer the brew. Other's ask if they might have some before the point at which I've decided to open the bottle, and I explain why I haven't yet opened it and ask if they prefer coffee early in the flight or late, that there isn't enough for all of us to have both. Anytime I pour a cup for myself, unless it's the last cup, I offer it around.

My first officer this month is one I hadn't flown with before and don't know well. We'd all had one cup of coffee already, and not long after that, while I was busy with paperwork, he simply leaned out of his seat and reached across the console to my side and picked up the Thermos from beside my knee.

I didn't think before reacting. I dropped my pen and grabbed the vacuum bottle and said in a hard voice, "Ask first."

The intensity of my reaction shocked and angered the first officer and surprised even me. The flight engineer quickly found something to do at his desk behind us.

The first-ever breach of tradition and protocol of the coffee ritual seemed at first to be nothing more than bad manners, but it was not. We were simply raised in different parts of the country with different traditions of social behavior.

Coffee rules: part two

The atmosphere in the cockpit was tense after I rebuked my copilot for helping himself to my coffee. He'd not flown with me before last month and had assumed my Thermos bottle was common provender, just as a bag of popcorn or a bunch of grapes would be.

I felt bad for having lost my temper and was surprised that I had done so. Perhaps subconsciously, I resent the fact that others who can't be bothered to carry their own coffee with them are more than willing to drink mine.

I apologized to Gary and explained what had set me off. Then I offered him a refill, but he refused it.

What to do? Even though our month of flying together was almost over, hard feelings on an airplane flight deck don't contribute to safety. And I don't like making enemies.

I again said he was welcome to more coffee, that it had become an expected thing over the years that I always had coffee for all three of us, but that I ration it to be sure it will last the entire night. Gary just hadn't known the "rules". He relented and accepted a refill, and I felt a little better.

As I thought the incident over, it occurred to me that Gary's helping himself to something I considered mine was exactly the sort of thing a longtime friend of mine does. It drives me nuts, and Bob can't understand what all the fuss is about.

Then came sudden insight as I realized that Gary and Bob, though from different states, grew up not far from one another in the same distinct region of the country, a sparsely settled, upper Midwest region of hard Winters and harsh Summers, a region where cooperation among people, even strangers, is a rule of necessity and is accepted convention.

Light & Dark

I told Gary this, and he began talking about life in rural northern Nebraska, where doors aren't locked and where, if you need to use a phone, you head for the nearest house. If nobody is home, you go in anyway and use the phone.

I couldn't do that. I was raised with the understanding that closed door meant don't come in without knocking and being invited in. Privacy was valued and respected in the world I grew up in.

I told Gary that Bob will knock on my front door and immediately open it and walk inside to find me. Gary looked at me with an expression that said, "Yeah? So?"

Even if I knew someone was home, I wouldn't do that. If it were a good friend, I might open the door and yell "Hello" if no one responded to a knock, but I'd not go inside uninvited unless previously instructed to do so. Even then, and even if it were friend's house, I wouldn't feel comfortable doing that.

Bob will cheerfully lend a car or a boat. I, on the other hand am uncomfortable lending anything more complex than hammer or a rake. It's not a matter of manners good and bad It's a matter of culture.

The first time an American spacecraft linked with a Russian one, the astronauts were miffed when the cosmonauts refused to shake hands in the common hatch between the craft. The Americans thought the Russians were playing a power game wanting the greetings to be on their turf. But in Russian tradition, it's not proper to perform greetings in doorways. The Russians were simply trying to avoid a breach of good manners.

I told Gary that wars have started over less.

Japanese students, especially girls, living in American homes are sometimes thought to be disrespectful because they look down when speaking or when spoken to. But in Japan, looking into someone's eyes during conversation is rude. What is considered good manners in a crowded country is not the same as proper behavior in a land with plenty of physical and psychological elbowroom.

So next time someone says or does something that bugs me, I'll try to keep my cool long enough to consider whether it's bad manners or just different manners.

Meanwhile, I think I'll keep my Thermos where no one else can reach it.

Buddy: nearing the end

Cancer in people is one thing. It's something we bring upon ourselves for the most part—too much sun, too much smoke, too much rich food. And if we live long enough, something is going to get us, so cancer in people past a certain age is not necessarily a surprise. But my dog doesn't smoke or expose bare skin to the sun, and he's only eight years old.

Buddy has always been an energetic dog. I've been watching for signs of his slowing down the past couple of years because I don't want to let him hunt as hard as he wants to if it's more than he can stand. But even now, in his ninth season in the woods and field, he seems to feel no need to take life easy.

I didn't even notice the small lump just under the skin of his flank, a lump invisible in his silky hair. Our vet found it during a routine exam in August.

Buddy has had a couple of small bumps on his neck since he was a puppy. Stable, benign cysts that do no harm. The lump in his flank was larger than those. If it seemed to bother him or get in his way, we could have it taken out. I thought I'd have it done after this hunting season.

As it turned out, Buddy tore himself up following his nose through thorny brush in lava cliffs near Quincy on the first day of our quail hunt. He wasn't hurt seriously, but enough that it would not have been good to let him continue. So I called the vet and made an appointment for stitches the next day. And while we were at it, we might as well cut out that cyst.

To add to his problems, Buddy must have caught a Yellowjacket buzzing around his food dish. His cheek was swollen.

Light & Dark

The lump in his flank had been growing in my mind, just as any defect, once noticed, looms large. But its growth was not just in my perception, and the vet seemed surprised at the size of it. Perhaps I shouldn't have mentioned the bee sting. Perhaps if I hadn't unknowingly misled him, he would have been concerned about that swelling, too.

When I took Buddy in to get his staples out, the vet showed me the biopsy report. Cancer, a particularly fast-growing type of tumor that, once one appears, more are likely.

Meanwhile, Buddy's bee-stung cheek was still swollen, swollen more, if anything. So instead of bringing my dog home, I left him there to have the lump taken out of his cheek. It, too, was cancer.

The burden of sorrow and pain is all on me. Buddy doesn't know anything is wrong. Aside from whatever irritation a face full of staples may impart, he is unmoved by it all.

Maybe he notices that I pay more attention to him than before, give him treats more often, and let him ride along more often on trips to town, but if he does notice, he doesn't mention it. He didn't even seem surprised that I finally let him ride up front in the new truck.

And, softhearted being that I am, I demand less of him in the field. He's not a good grouse hunter because he has never realized that it does us no good for him to range a couple hundred yards out in woods too dense for me to see him or hear his bell beyond a few feet. But now, instead of constantly reminding him to hunt close, I let him do as he pleases, and, in the absence of my frequent reminders, he pays more attention to where I am and stays closer to the gun. I'll try hard to remember this with my next dog.

My next dog. That's a hard phrase to think on. I do not know how long it will be before the lumps appear faster than we can cut them out, before a tumor sprouts that cannot be removed. It may be weeks or months or years.

Because I don't know how long my fuzzy friend will be with me, I'll treat him every day as if it might be his last. I should have been doing that since the day I brought him home. And if I should treat my dog that way, perhaps I should also treat the people I love that way.

`aking a dream to the skies

Jsually it's the young who dream impossible dreams. Most
older folks give up before their hair is gray or gone, give up
.eir dreams and get on with the business of living. But not
ways.
t's not my dream I'm talking about. I've already realized many
' mine, and it's nice to occasionally see someone else fall
:adlong into his idea of heaven on Earth.
This particular dream-come-true strikes close to my own heart.
earned of its realization by e-mail, a most modern way to hear
the re-emergence of something that all but the oldest of us
gard as a quaint bit of aviation history.
The man's interest in radio broadcasting was evident when he
id I were in high school. He went on to a distinguished career
television journalism, only to have it cut short by today's cold-
ooded, shortsighted manifestations of corporate callousness
.lled downsizing.
What to do? Too old to start at the bottom of some other ladder,
o young to sit and watch the world go by. With little
.portunity to be practical, he headed in another direction toward
. almost forgotten dream. He bought an airplane and learned to
.
n the early days of aviation, fliers bought surplus stick-and-
'oric Jennies and other primitive discards and made their livings
.rnstorming—flying around the country, landing in fields near
.iall towns, and selling rides to those who came out to see the
'ing machine, a few dollars for a few minutes to see their world
'm the sky.
\ few people still do that, if only as a hobby. I became incurably
fected with the need to fly after a ten-minute ride in an old
'plane more than twenty years ago. The pilot was a dentist by
ide but an aviator at heart.

123

Light & Dark

My former classmate spent still more of his generous severance package (corporations, like people, try to buy their way to clear consciences) on a modern reproduction of a 1929 Great Lakes, an open-cockpit biplane with all the dash and élan of those early flying machines, but built of modern materials to modern standards of reliability and safety. He learned to fly loops and rolls, how to play in the sky with the glee of the child in him that decades of proper adulthood hadn't completely smothered.

But pleasure shared is pleasure doubled. Surely there would be plenty of people in a huge California city that would pay a few dollars to ride the wind in goggles and leather helmet. Of course these being modern times, insurance would be a necessity, and that almost killed the dream. Liability costs were impossibly high.

But, not being one to quit so close after coming so far, he finally found insurance at a reasonable rate and hung out his shingle.

Well, this being the threshold of the twenty-first century, he did more than hang out a shingle. He has a telephone and e-mail and a site on the Internet. He flies not out of pastures but from an airport.

A ride costs considerably more than what I paid years ago although, adjusted for inflation, the rates my friend charges may be less than those of the earliest days of barnstorming.

I confess a bit of envy. The wind in his cockpit is flavored with orange blossoms and mown hay; in mine, the dehydrated pressurized air is devoid of fragrance. The sound in his ear, once he clears the control tower's space, is the song of wind in wires and the thunder of pistons, while I hear amplified voices and the shriek of thin air on aluminum and glass.

He sent me a note the other day. He advised me, that when life gets too hectic, too chaotic, to go rent a little airplane. Getting up in the sky helps keep perspective, he's discovered. Sometimes he flies to keep his feet on the ground.

[It was too good to last, of course. After a couple of years, the insurance company was absorbed by a bigger one that, for no discernible reason, reduced liability coverage to almost nothing, and a thriving business, a soaring dream, crashed to Earth.]

On faith, facts, and truth

Facts are solid, as cold and disinterested as numbers. A jury composed of computers would render only unanimous verdicts. Facts don't leave room for argument.

Truth is what we make of facts. Different people interpret facts in different ways, depending on their own knowledge, experience, and desires. Jurors seeking truthful interpretations of facts often disagree with one another. While facts do not change, truths derived from them change as more facts are discovered.

Faith simply ignores inconvenient facts and remains whatever the believer wants it to be.

We can discuss facts without emotion, without feeling that we have to defend something we have a personal investment in. While we discuss facts, we argue over truth. Even in a trial in which facts are not disputed, each side tries to convince the jury that its own interpretation of the facts is the true one.

Politics owes its existence to differing interpretations of fact. Differences of opinion can lead to war to the degree that war is an extension of politics. But while disagreements over truths may lead to war, arguments over faith can lead to the fanatical excesses of holy war.

In my job, I work with two other people I may not know at all. We fly for hours a couple of feet apart and often have meals together on layovers. It's important that there be no animosity among flight crews. Anger is incompatible with cooperation, and lack of cooperation leads to accidents. Pilots tend to be strong willed, opinionated people, so the potential for conflict is high.

I do a couple of things when with crews I don't know to learn what subjects to avoid in flight. The simplest is to simply listen to them. An absence of profanity in casual speech may be an indicator of strong religious faith. I also pay attention to what they do in restaurants when our food is served. If someone bows his head for a moment before beginning to eat, I remain silent and still, not out of shared faith but out of respect, and I resolve to avoid subjects that might challenge his faith.

The most heated discussion I encountered among crewmembers exploded into a fierce, near-hysterical diatribe in a hotel lobby. The man would not permit any counter-argument. He would not even listen to demands that he lower his voice and control his language. The subject was political, but the fire in his heart was faith.

The jury in OJ Simpson's criminal trial heard the same facts the rest of us did, but the truth the jury reached was not the same truth that most Americans derived. Because of the jurors' backgrounds and experiences, they could lend little weight to some facts that most of us considered insurmountable.

A district attorney in Texas accepted a new perception of truth when facts indicated that the state's new law permitting citizens to carry guns did not create the bloodbath in the streets he argued it would. "I'm eating a lot of crow on this issue," he said. "It's not something I necessarily like to do, but I'm doing it on this." A rational man, he recognized that what he believed to be true did not fit facts and changed his opinion.

By contrast, it is an article of faith at Handgun Control, Inc. that the most onerous restriction on gun ownership is justified if it saves even one life. When confronted with a new study from the University of Chicago that concludes that allowing citizens to carry concealed weapons reduces crime, including murder, an HCI board member's response was that a mere five- to ten percent decrease in brutal crime wasn't enough reason to justify allowing citizens to carry guns. He couldn't change his opinion because he is operating on faith, a factually insupportable belief that guns are bad. "We have to do away with the guns," he said.

Truth recognizes facts and incorporates them. Faith is under no obligation to do so.

Let the kid be a kid, Grandpa

The hardest part of introducing a five-year-old boy to trout fishing is getting him out of the store before he pokes someone's eye out with his new spinning rod. The second hardest part is remembering this is all for the boy's enjoyment, not the old man's.

My grandson had been practicing casting with his mother's old rod in his San Jose driveway and talking about going fishing with Grandpa. Well, why not?

I thought the long road trip would have tired him out, which just goes to show how long it's been since I was a little boy on the eve of a fishing trip. I did tell him Grandma gets up early, and he could, too. And I told him he could wake me if I was still asleep, but not until the sun came up. I read him a story and he went to bed.

Bright orange light had just flooded the house when I awoke to a gentle tapping on my shoulder and opened my eyes to see the bright eyes and wide grin of my fully dressed grandson. He was ready.

We loaded up Tim's new tackle box with lures and hooks and the usual assortment of goodies that clutter up tackle boxes in basements and garages across America. We drove to Lake Sutherland and put our small boat in.

The object of the expedition was for Tim to catch a fish. Fishing is pretty boring until that first fish is caught. After that, well, I'd let his parents contend with any resulting obsession.

Light & Dark

The object of the expedition, from the little boy's point of view was simply to have fun.

I'd forgotten what a short attention span a small boy has. Tim was ready to quit fishing and drive the boat after about three minutes. Grouchy old Grandpa insisted we fish for a while first.

American humor is full of ironic jokes about our insistence on enjoying ourselves, even if we make ourselves miserable in the process. I tried to keep that in mind, and when Tim's interest waned, I tried to remember that the object was for him to have an enjoyable time in his own way, not necessarily in the old man's way. So we reeled in and putted around the lake for a while, Tim at the tiller with a grin on his face.

The strike, when it came, was on my rod, not Tim's, but I handed it to him, and the fish got off as I did so. It was past time to go home, but the fever was ignited, in me, if not in the boy. We continued to troll under the trees along the bank.

Too bad he hadn't felt the thrill of a fish on his line, but there were more days in the week to come. On the other hand...

We drove up the Elwha to a spot above Altaire where at least one or two small trout always strike, although I'd never fished it with anything other than flies. I helped Tim cast and retrieve his spinner with no response from trout, but one did jump high for a flying bug. The day was not lost!

We raced each other back to the truck and rigged up my fly rod. We didn't catch a fish, but I realized Tim would probably get the hang of fly fishing in about ten minutes.

We got home late for supper and Tim fell asleep before he got his clothes off. Grandma was mildly disgusted that I'd kept him out so late. "He's only five!"

And so he is. As I carried him to bed and tucked him in, I silently apologized to him and hoped I hadn't soured him on going fishing, or anywhere else, with Grandpa.

I guess I didn't. He tapped me awake as soon as the sky was light. He'd gotten up, showered, dressed, and was ready to go. He's at my elbow as I write this, telling me to hurry up.

We're going to only one small lake today. The guidebook says it's full of brook trout and a perfect place to teach children to fish. So we'll do that now, and when Tim is through for the day, we'll come home. I'll indulge my own obsession on my own time.

Heaven's Gate? Beam 'em up

don't understand why the mass suicide of thirty-nine religious
fanatics in California was and continues to be such a huge
tory. The members of Heaven's Gate weren't murdered, after all,
nd the average third-world bus crash kills more people. It's not
s if there is a shortage of human beings on the planet, or even in
alifornia. Our national horror seems especially strange in light
f the fact that polls indicate we are overwhelmingly religious.

Some wag has said that the difference between a religion and a
ult is that a religion has a college with a football team. That flip
mark oversimplifies the distinction, perhaps, but it does prompt
irther thought.

Throughout history, comets have stimulated human imagination
ir beyond questions of physics and astronomy. Comets are
ortents from heaven, or maybe from hell. Or, in this case, from
homever runs the show for Heaven's Gate.

To most of us, the idea that, after physical death, our spirits will
e transported to a spacecraft "hiding" behind Hale-Bopp is
idicrous. But, given the number of otherwise normal people who
elieve UFOs are spaceships crewed by aliens who routinely
bduct human beings, perform perverse examinations and
xperiments on them—sexual and otherwise—and return them to
ieir homes, perhaps the beliefs of Heaven's Gate aren't absurd
t all.

If someone with an unusually rational mind were raised to

adulthood with no exposure to religion, no discussion of spirituality, and not even casual contact with superstition, what would he make of such human beliefs as a cult's beliefs, or Christianity, or fear of black cats?

To such a person—Star Trek's Mr Spock comes to mind—the fact that hotels leave out thirteen when numbering floors would seem absurd. The idea that the appearance of a comet was a heavenly sign that it was time to tuck a five-dollar bill and a couple of quarters into one's pocket and drink a fatal cocktail to leave the body and move to a "higher level" on a flying saucer would surely be incomprehensible.

But what might our supremely rational person think of the idea that a man allowed himself to be killed and came back to life three days later, spoke to a few people, and then disappeared? When told the man did this to save subsequent generations from after-death consequences of sin, would he find that any more reasonable than the tenets of Heaven's Gate? What might this person think of other beliefs that cannot be substantiated by logic or mathematics or science?

Considering that each of the many branches, divisions, and sects of modern Christianity considers its view to be, if not the only "correct" one, the one closest to God's concept of a Christian church, and considering that among these sects are Catholics, Lutherans, and people who commune with poisonous snakes, our rational outsider might be forgiven if he had difficulty determining the difference between a religion and a cult.

Every few years, somebody gets the word from God that the end of the world is coming on some particular day a year or two down the road. Usually the result is little more than embarrassment and perhaps financial ruin when the holy man's believers give away all they own and sit down in the desert to wait for the final dawn, a dawn that proves indistinguishable from the ones before and the ones after.

The Heaven's Gate members undoubtedly believed in their vision of eternity at least as strongly as the average Methodist or Presbyterian. Maybe they believed more strongly, or maybe they were simply impatient.

In my mind, I see our Mr Spock consider all these things, then slowly shake his head and walk away.

Global warming is nothing new

I listen with bemusement to the hot argument over global warming. The lesser focus is on the mostly scientific contention that the planet's temperature is rising.

Most of the heat is generated by the mostly political argument that it's our fault, that if modern civilization weren't interfering with Eden on Earth, that if we selfish Americans especially weren't burning so much oil, smoking so much tobacco, and eating so much fast food, there would be no problem with climate.

The unstated assumption of the alarmists seems to be that this trend toward higher average temperature is abnormal and bad. Ice will melt, seas will rise, prairies will become deserts, and real estate prices will rise in Canada and Siberia. Well, so what? Maybe they always have. Maybe they always will.

What makes any of us think that today's climate is the norm and a constant? Ice Ages have come and gone without any help from us. Even in recorded history, world temperatures have risen and fallen in cycles within cycles over decades and centuries.

Norse sagas of exploration were considered fiction not many years ago by people who should have known better. Grapes on the coast of Canada? Must be translation errors—Vinland was really in Virginia. Year-round farming in Greenland? Impossible. Too cold. It's too cold now, but it was warmer a thousand years ago.

131

Light & Dark

What makes us think that Earth's violent evolution suddenly became stable about the time we arrived and will remain so forever? The planet's history is of continual—if not continuous— change, of land becoming ocean and then land again, of mountain ranges rising from plains and wearing down to level ground, of deserts becoming verdant and then arid again, of lava flows covering areas as large as states. The north magnetic pole occasionally swaps ends with the south.

Ah, but that was millions of years ago!

The last of untold numbers of Ice Ages ended—or appears to us to have "ended"—only a few thousand years ago. To suggest that the glaciers will not come back to add another cycle to the record seems extremely egocentric.

Perhaps this global warming, if it is a long-term trend and not a short sub-cycle, is what melts the glaciers back to end each Ice Age. Or perhaps it is periods of global warming that create the conditions that cause the ice sheets to form in the Arctic and slide down over our end of the Earth.

Our planet has been changing for billions of years and we've been observing it for only a moment.

It is observed fact that, since we've been measuring such things, our planet's average temperature has been rising. But we've been measuring for such a short time, how can we apply those observations of a few decades to periods of thousands and millions of years? It would be like living deep in a cave since birth and then, on a pleasant April morning, looking outside for the first time ever and concluding after a moment's observation that the planet is always cool and damp. And then, as the day progresses, the observer becomes alarmed by the ominous trend toward evaporating dew and rising temperature.

Perhaps there are more cycles than we, in our moment of observation, can be aware of. We know that day follows night and that Fall follows Summer. These are cycles so short that we live through many and are accustomed to them. We would become alarmed if the sun stood still at noon or if Spring never came.

The familiar cycles of day and night, of and, seem right to us, seem a natural cycle of rebirth and renewal. Perhaps recurring cycles of global warming and glaciation are the same thing on a much larger scale, natural and inevitable, and maybe, in the greater scheme of things, good.

Giving thanks at Christmas

This is an unusual Christmas at our house. Not an unpleasant day, just different. Barb and I are at home, but nobody else is here with us.

There are gifts under the tree, of course, but not many. We've reached the point in life where we've acquired more than what we really need and are trying to reduce the clutter in our lives. Most of our friends and family are also burdened with more than they need, so, except for grandsons and nephews and nieces, we've pretty much given up the feeling of obligation to swap neckties and sweaters at Christmas.

With only a few gifts to buy it should be easy to be watchful through the year for gifts just right for the handful of young people on our lists. It is, for Barb.

You might think that a reasonably intelligent person such as I would realize, after half a century and more of seeing Christmas come every year and on the same day every year, that when the calendar is turned to the last page and the date is in two digits, Christmas is very near. But, two days before Christmas, long after Barb has bought, wrapped, and mailed, gifts to the kids in her side of the family, I was only half finished with gift selection, as usual.

I got our Christmas letter off late, too, in spite of last year's vow to have it written by Thanksgiving and mailed soon after.

When I was growing up in Colorado, Christmas often meant a trip to Texas to celebrate with all the grandparents and aunts and uncles and cousins on both sides of the family. We did the traveling because my parents were the only ones in either family who lived outside the home state.

Until a few years ago—it seems much less time than years ago—our daughter was the center of our Christmas whether we stayed home or spent the holiday with relatives.

Barb grew up in Washington. Her mother, brother, sister, and several aunts and uncles still live near Puget Sound. Spending part of the holidays with her family is easy, so we often do that. But not this year. Our daughter and grandsons will be with us for a few days, though not until after Christmas.

I've been extraordinarily lucky with holidays and work. I have never had to spend Christmas away from home in a hotel in Newark or Cleveland. I don't have to work Christmas Day this year, either, but I have to leave in the afternoon for my commute to Cincinnati. So we aren't going anywhere today. After Christmas Eve services with friends, Christmas morning is ours alone.

Not quite alone, of course. Barb and I are the only two people in the house, but our cat yowls its wake-up call when it hears the timed coffee maker begin to burble. After a romp around the yard, all three dogs gallop into the house, as usual, and slide through turns on the hardwood floors as they check all the rooms and corners to be sure they're not overlooking something that wasn't there the night before—a mislaid cookie from a late-night snack, perhaps.

The bird feeders on the deck are crowded on this and most Winter mornings with Finches and Juncos and Grosbeaks, and an occasional Jay or Starling. So, counting dogs and birds and the cat, we aren't really alone.

As there are no small, wide-eyed hyperexcited children in the house, we relax with unhurried morning coffee and listen to Christmas music on the radio. We watch the holy morning brighten over the bay and think about things central to the holiday, things often lost in the hustle and bustle.

It's time for us to give thanks, we few in the world who have food to eat and a place to call home and a reasonable assurance that we and our loved ones will have these things tomorrow and the day after. It's time to reflect and to give thanks to whatever god or spirit or star we believe in that we are, through accident of birthplace and little else, so very, very lucky.

Buddy: the end

The recurring realization that my freckled English Setter was approaching his tenth birthday always startled me. Buddy had the energy and enthusiasm of a pup. Perhaps, I thought, he'd live to the far edge of canine mortality.

Some people deny themselves the joy of owning a pet because they are afraid to face its eventual death. If they can't have the pleasure without the pain, they'll do without both. I would not enjoy so empty a life. Others say that anyone who can't shoot his dog when the time comes shouldn't own a dog, but I am not so hard a man as that.

When I took Buddy in to have a lump on his leg removed and analyzed, he looked more comical that usual. His upper lip was swollen on one side of his mouth. He'd finally caught one of the yellowjackets that sometimes buzzed around his food dish, I thought. But the swelling was still there a week later when I took him in to get the staples from his surgery removed. The knot on his leg was cancerous, a malignancy all but impossible to cure. There was no practical treatment but to cut the tumors out as they appeared. So, instead of taking him home, I left him there to have the second one cut out of his lip.

Then, a few months ago, his nose began to swell, not much and not fast, but right where the surgeon had feared some cancer cells might have remained.

I'd decided long before that I was not going to whittle tumors off my dog until there was nothing left. I'd do what I could as long as he was not incapacitated or in great pain, but no more. I'd want no more and no less for myself.

After several weeks with no increase in the swelling, I'd begun to allow myself to hope there'd be one more hunting season in him. This season would be his, not mine. We'd spend as much time as possible hunting pheasant and quail in the sage land that he loves east of the Cascades. I'd let deer and elk take a back seat this year. He enjoyed riding in our new canoe, so I took him as often as I could, a flop-eared figurehead in the bow, eyes on the horizon searching for new adventure.

Then his nose began to swell again.

In the two weeks my wife and I were away traveling, his nose grew larger and new lumps erupted under the skin on his chest and leg. He chewed a tumor off his ribs just before we got home.

I could not go away to work again and leave him declining so fast. I called the vet and said it was time for Buddy's last shot.

He jumped into his seat in the truck, eager, as always, to go for a ride. If he noticed my tears, he was gentleman enough not to mention them. When I turned into the clinic's parking lot, he started shivering with apprehension, as he'd only come to do since the first time he'd had to stay overnight and I'd left him. I'd already decided to ask the doctor to come outside to the truck so Buddy wouldn't be afraid, and, while we waited, I ran him through his hand-signal drills in the parking lot.

This is more like it! Hunting stuff! He forgot where he was as he ran the drills on silent command, and when I signaled him to the truck, he jumped into the back and sat down, tail wagging, excited again and happy to be alive.

His first shot was a tranquilizer, one he didn't notice, one that would make the last one unnoticeable. I drove around to the back of the clinic, away from passersby, and as we waited for the first drug to slow him down, I sent him into a patch of brush and grass to "find the birds" one last time.

He looked into my eyes and didn't flinch when the needle slipped into a vein. I held him as he lay down and died. His eyes are forever sightless now, and so, for a time, were mine.

If your book store does not have this book, please order direct. Photocopy this page or write to:

Light & Dark
Peninsula Daily News
PO Box 1330
Port Angeles WA 98362

$10.00 per copy plus $3.00 S&H for the first copy.
Add $1.00 for each of the second, third, and fourth copies. We pay shipping on orders of five or more.
Washington State residents: Add $.79 sales tax per copy.
Make checks payable to <u>Peninsula Daily News</u>

Name_____

Address_____

City_____ State/Prov_____ Zip/Postal Code____

Country_____ Phone_____

☐ VISA ☐ Mastercard   Account #_____

Expiration date_____

Books @$10 x _____   S&H (\$6 max.) _____   WA Res Tx \$.79/copy _____   T¼